THE
PLAYBOOK
for
MIDDLE SCHOOL
TEACHERS

D0813743

THE PLAYBOOK
for
MIDDLE SCHOOL TEACHERS

LOIS RINALDI

ARCHWAY
PUBLISHING

Copyright © 2016 Lois Rinaldi.

All rights reserved. No part of this book may be used or reproduced by any means,
graphic, electronic, or mechanical, including photocopying, recording, taping or
by any information storage retrieval system without the written permission of the
author except in the case of brief quotations embodied in critical articles and reviews.

Archway Publishing books may be ordered through booksellers or by contacting:

Archway Publishing
1663 Liberty Drive
Bloomington, IN 47403
www.archwaypublishing.com
1 (888) 242-5904

Because of the dynamic nature of the Internet, any web addresses or
links contained in this book may have changed since publication and
may no longer be valid. The views expressed in this work are solely those
of the author and do not necessarily reflect the views of the publisher,
and the publisher hereby disclaims any responsibility for them.

Any people depicted in stock imagery provided by Thinkstock are models,
and such images are being used for illustrative purposes only.
Certain stock imagery © Thinkstock.

ISBN: 978-1-4808-3400-2 (sc)
ISBN: 978-1-4808-3401-9 (e)

Library of Congress Control Number: 2016910885

Print information available on the last page.

Archway Publishing rev. date: 10/4/2016

CONTENTS

ACKNOWLEDGMENTS

I want to thank my family for their constant encouragement and unending support throughout the writing process. Their creative ideas, logical advice, and incredible patience were invaluable.

I want to thank Mary Pappalardo and Vicki Valley, two amazing teachers, for their practical suggestions and editorial support. I also want to thank Carra Pappalardo for her editing expertise and helpful suggestions for my manuscript.

Finally, I want to thank my former students who planted the seed for this book. They suggested that I write this book – divulging all their mischievous shenanigans in the classroom. I hope they enjoy reading about themselves in the book.

Chapter 1

Introduction

> It is the supreme art of the teacher to awaken
> joy in creative expression and knowledge.
> –Albert Einstein

This book is a compilation of my best advice for new middle school teachers. I taught English in middle school for more than thirty years in both public and independent schools, and I want to share effective strategies with you to help you build confidence and achieve success. Had I known this information prior to beginning my own career, it would have made my career much easier to navigate. The experiences I am sharing are particular to my teaching experience, and they may not speak directly to yours; however, this playbook for middle school teachers is essential for managing your career and meeting the challenges of the profession.

The Playbook for Middle School Teachers covers significant events that occur throughout a typical school year to help you keep one step ahead of the students in order to survive your first year of teaching. Students are savvy about how unaware new teachers are regarding the shenanigans that students are ready to use on an unsuspecting neophyte. They collaborate before class on how to make teachers the brunt of their jokes. To be informed is to be prepared.

You will learn how to manage field trips, navigate Parents' Night, and handle conferences. I also address technological issues such as cellphones, social media, and the Internet. Technology is a major part of students' lives, and learning how to incorporate it appropriately or *not* into the school day is essential to your success and your students' success in middle school. In addition, you will learn the importance of listening to the wisdom of your experienced colleagues and how to handle bullying incidents and cheating situations. Finally, you will learn how to manage your career as a professional in the field of teaching.

Teaching is one of the most rewarding professions on the planet. It will not make you rich in worldly terms, but it will make you rich in wonderful memories. The liveliness of youth with their curiosity for learning and incredible energy will bring you joy for many years to come.

CHAPTER 2

PREPARATION

Before anything else, preparation
is the key to success.
–Alexander Graham Bell

In order to have a successful school year, preparation is essential. You had the summer to relax and rejuvenate your mind, body, and spirit in order to face the challenges of the upcoming year. Now is the time to set the stage for a successful school year. The classroom environment you create should be emotionally welcoming, academically stimulating, and functionally compatible for your students. You are trying to create a wow factor on day one. Students who feel excited to learn in the classroom climate that you have created will look forward to coming to your classes every day throughout the school year.

There are several important steps to take prior to opening day:

1. **Organize the Books.** When you arrive at your classroom after the summer, be ready to unpack your books and organize your room. Place the books in neat piles in your classroom with book numbers, which you assign beginning with number one and so on. Use a black, indelible Sharpie marker to write the numbers on the closed pages of the book. Keep a list of the numbers and later write your students' names next to the book numbers; the list should be kept in a separate file on your computer for easy access

at the end of the year. When you collect the books in June, you can be sure that students are handing in the book that they were assigned in September, not someone else's book. Students are known to try to hand in another student's book if they have lost their own. They do not want a bill sent to their parents for the cost of the book, which will undoubtedly require an explanation on their part about how and when they lost their text. However, with accurate records, you will be able to keep a student honest, and the school administrative assistant will be able to order a new book with the replacement fee. Textbooks are extremely costly today, and with school budgets under scrutiny, your perfect record keeping will be commended.

2. **Decorate the Classroom**. The walls of your classroom should be decorated with inspirational posters and academic posters. Inspirational posters will keep up students' spirits during difficult learning situations. Academic posters such as mathematical formulas or parts of speech will help students learn and reference key information. Students will enjoy viewing the posters daily as they enter your classroom. Colorful posters strategically placed throughout the classroom will also create a friendly environment, and you should change the posters each trimester for variety. For example, if the students are studying short stories in the fall, have posters of famous authors and the elements of the short story for them to view. You might also add posters that feature punctuation rules and the basic elements of writing a five-paragraph essay on the wall for easy reference. There is nothing more pleasing to the eye than purposefully placed posters for students to observe while they are sitting in a classroom.

3. **Create Bulletin Boards**. One area of your classroom should have a bulletin board where you can post your schedule

for extra help, the classroom rules, athletic schedules, and theatrical schedules. This bulletin board should be in the front of the room near the door, where all students will have easy and quick access to this information. Be sure this information is updated weekly. Each week, assign one of your advisees to be the bulletin-board specialist, and he or she will gain experience in organizational management. Your role as advisor is to have all the information ready for your advisee to place on the bulletin board. This advisee/specialist will then place the information on the bulletin board in designated categories (e.g. drama or game schedules) and keep everyone up to date on all activities throughout the school for that particular week. Rotate this bulletin-board-specialist position to each of your advisees during each trimester. At the end of a trimester, reward your advisees with a cupcake surprise or a pizza lunch. This will be a memorable experience for them.

4. **Arrange the Desks**. Arrange your desks and/or tables in interesting patterns throughout the year. You can begin the year with the seminar style, with desks or tables forming a giant rectangle. You can sit or stand in the middle of one of the sides of the rectangle to teach. However, if you feel your students have become too talkative with this arrangement, change to rows of desks or tables – a more traditional style. Your desk can be situated in one corner of the room. Never sit at your desk unless you are correcting tests after school. Walking around the room during class gives you a clear view of who is paying attention and who is surfing the Internet. You can also try placing desks or tables in small circles for reading groups. Any creative style is fine as long as the students are engaged in the lesson.

5. **Prepare a Syllabus**. Once your room looks student-ready, prepare your lessons for the next two weeks and make

copies of handouts. Create a syllabus for the year, so students will have a clear overview of what they will learn in your subject during each trimester. Try to memorize as many names as you can by using last year's yearbook. You can put a face to a name before the students arrive. If you have students with the same first name, call them by initials (for example, Thomas Paine becomes TP and Thomas Jefferson becomes TJ.)

6. **Create a Class Expectations Handout.** Create a "Class Expectations" handout that explains your classroom rules, homework policy, grading policy, and absentee-makeup procedures. On the back of this document, place a syllabus of your course for the year. Students and parents need to have a clear understanding of the expectations for your class. Give this handout to students on the first day of class, and clearly state that a parent must sign the document. Emphasize that the return date is tomorrow's class. Students will forget to return the document unless you expect to have it returned the following day. Documents like this can sit at the bottom of a book bag for an entire school year if you are not vigilant about the return date. Check each student's name on a prepared student list to be sure all students are compliant with your request. Store these documents in a safe place. Should any problems regarding student performance arise throughout the year, you can refer to these documents, which everyone was apprised of at the beginning of the year.

7. **Post Homework on Website.** Finally, be sure your homework website is available for viewing on the school website. Teach new students how to navigate your website. Update your posted assignments for the week by Sunday night at 6 p.m. Then students can begin to fill in their daily planners on Sunday night and maybe even get a jumpstart

on homework for the week. Parents will sing your praises for your punctuality and professionalism.

Preparation is the key to a positive and productive school year. Students will receive a crystal-clear message about your preparedness and professionalism just by observing your organizational skills and your classroom management. By handing out a syllabus for the year and books on the first day of school, students will know that you are prepared and in control of your classroom. With this kind of thorough preparation, you will have clearly demonstrated your expectations to your students for the academic year.

Chapter 3

Day One

How does the school year typically begin?

Late August seems like a welcomed relief for parents and *the challenge of a lifetime* for new teachers. Teachers – set your radar. The exhilarating excitement of the students on day one of the new school year cannot be misconstrued as a portent of what will follow. Students are socially starved when they return to school because they have not seen their BFFs (Best Friends Forever) all summer. Most important on the first day is screaming, hugging, and taking photos on their cellphones. Catching up on what happened last summer is a close second. After this necessary middle school drama subsides, classes may begin. Do not mistake their enthusiasm in the hallway to be transferred to your classroom. Make no mistake about it; the social life of middle school students supersedes their academic pursuits. It is most helpful to have supportive parents and administrative support to frequently remind students that the main reason they are in school is to take advantage of the excellent educational opportunities that are available to them. Most students will pay lip service to your rationale about why they are in school and smile like a Cheshire cat. Don't be fooled by their relatively good behavior on day one.

Here are a few caveats for the first day of school.

1. I know you have heard this said in Education 101: "Don't smile until Christmas."
    Restate that to be: "Don't smile until June."

"Why?" you might ask.

Middle school students perceive your smile to mean a license to laugh uncontrollably, talk incessantly, and act disrespectfully. They have *no* filters, and your smile is a license to fool around repeatedly throughout the year.

2. Give a lecture about how important their reputation is throughout their school years and later in life. It never hurts to put a little fear in them about what others might think about them right from the start. Middle school students place a very high value on what others think of them – not only their peers but also their teachers.

3. Hand out a *Class Expectations* form with a syllabus and make sure their parents sign it. File it for future use. It is a contract among the students, the parents, and the teacher for the entire year. It is also a document that you can use to reiterate your expectations should problems occur during the school year. You can reiterate these expectations on Parents' Night. This night is *showtime* for you to appeal to and win over the hearts and minds of the parents.

4. Hand out books and expect them to be covered with a book sock by the next class. Don't be surprised when students use these book socks as hats at the end of the year after they return their books. These book socks will have a year's worth of germs on them, but it does not seem to matter to middle school students. Fun is paramount to them.

5. Lockers are required to be locked. When handing out locks, perseverating on this fact will curb future problems. When students state that someone took an item from their locker, you should ask if their locker was locked. The answer will most likely be, "No." To expect that an unlocked locker will receive no *visitors* is totally naïve and foolish, but this reality evades students in middle school. In addition, be sure students memorize their combos and use their lockers.

Beware of the locks that appear locked but are not fully locked, for a quick open and retrieval of books on the run. Keep a master list of combos for those students with short-term memories. You will inevitably be the go-to person for locker combos during the year. Students will be very upbeat and excited to learn on the first day of school. It would be wonderful to bottle up this new energy and enthusiasm for an entire school year.

One of the most wonderful classes I ever taught was a seventh grade class at an independent school in Connecticut. I had been teaching there for twenty-eight years, but this class was unique. They greeted me in the morning with a smile and thanked me for teaching them at the end of class each day. Can you believe such cordiality? They were eager to learn and to perform at their maximum potential. They actually had a quest for knowledge that I had not seen in many years. Somewhere under the stars, these children were born and landed in my class.

I was hoping that the first day of school would be a premonition of things to come. All students were sparkling clean and well groomed in their new clothes. No one was out of dress code. Boys wore khaki pants and colored polo jerseys, and girls wore a similar style of clothing. Their book bags were packed with new notebooks, folders, pens, note cards, and computers, just waiting for the school year to begin. Who could ask for more?

It was a typical first day in all my classes with the distribution of books and the clarification of class rules. Students were on their best behavior as books were handed out and classroom rules were explained. Everyone was exemplifying the best behavior I had ever seen in my many years of teaching. Frankly, I was a little suspicious that this stellar behavior was only going to last one day. However, at the end of the first day, I was amazed to see that the classroom was not strewn with remnants of the students' books, clothes, and backpacks – hopefully a portent of things to come. All my advisees had taken their belongings home that evening in preparation for the next day.

As they walked out the door, they all said, "Have a great evening, Mrs. R!"

I courteously replied to each of my advisees, "I hope you have a wonderful evening as well."

I was absolutely delighted with the prospect of a fantastic year with these amazing students. Was I looking through rose-colored glasses? Was this class truly as awesome as the previous teachers had purported? To date their behavior was commendable, and I only wished for more of the same for the rest of the year.

I had bus duty that day, and I recognized many students from last year who were boarding the bus. I carefully checked each student's name on the bus list before anyone was allowed to board the bus. It was great to see how tall many of my former students had grown during the summer; they also showed signs of maturity as we chatted about their summer experiences and their expectations for the school year. After the bus departed, I was pleasantly surprised with the events of the first day of school and walked back to the middle school to plan the next day's lesson.

Believe it or not, the first day and the rest of the week were like the movie *Groundhog Day*. The students were prepared for class, and their behavior was totally respectful. They were engaged in the learning process, thanked me for teaching them after class, and wished me a wonderful evening. Who could ask for anything more?

As I continue writing this book, it is important to mention that the students in the previous anecdote willingly shared some techniques with me that they employed to create mischievous behavior during the school year. Other methods of misbehavior were learned from many years in the classroom. "Forewarned is forearmed," is an excellent proverb to adhere to when it comes to disciplining a class. It is always wise to be knowledgeable about the intentions of your students, so you can be prepared to deal with disruptive behavior in an effective manner. Then students will respect your authority in the classroom, and they will learn the parameters of classroom behavior. Once these boundaries have been established, real learning can occur. No one can learn in a chaotic, noisy, disrespectful environment. You owe it to your students to create a classroom in which all students have the opportunity to learn in a relaxed and respectful environment.

CHAPTER 4

FIELD TRIPS

Knowing the steps to planning a field trip will determine either the success or failure of a trip. The most important part of planning any trip is to check the middle school calendar to be sure no other trip has been planned for the same day. Check the all-school calendar to be sure that an important school event has not already been scheduled. Once this day is established as a school day with no conflicts, and the principal has given his or her permission for the trip, the designated teacher should talk to the scheduler at the bus company to establish a date and time for the trip.

Step 1. The class dean is often the person responsible for making the arrangements for the trip. The class dean must explain the detailed expectations of the itinerary to the bus company, get a confirmation on the price, and arrange for payment. To ensure that the trip runs smoothly, always call the bus company two weeks before the trip to confirm the date and time of the trip. You never want to be responsible for 50 students and five chaperones or more – excited and ready to leave for an educational field trip – and have a bus no show. If that happens, your reputation will be damaged.

Step 2. Many schools have a basic form that parents sign at the beginning of the school year, giving permission for their child to attend school field trips. This saves a great deal of paperwork and time for both teachers and parents.

Step 3. One *very* important piece of information that needs to be taken on every field trip is the contact information for each child's parent or guardian, which is usually kept in the school office with the principal. This information about the child and his or her family can be placed in an electronic database if the school chooses to do so. If not, then one of the teachers on the trip needs to be responsible for securing these forms before leaving for the trip; the teacher who is responsible for these contact forms *must* carry these forms during the entire trip. If a child has to go to the hospital, then parents must be notified of the incident and give permission for any medical procedures. Parents are also asked at the beginning of the year to submit an updated physical for their child, which contains any allergies of which teachers must be aware. For example, if a child has a severe reaction to a bee sting and goes into shock, the head teacher on the field trip must have the EpiPen available and know how to use it – ASAP. Then they must call 911. This type of training on how to use an EpiPen is given to all teachers and administrators at the beginning of every school year – usually by the school nurse.

Step 4. Another *very* important part of planning a field trip is to let the cafeteria know what day you will be taking the trip and how many students will need a bag lunch for that day. Students are often given a lunch menu two weeks before the trip and are asked what kind of sandwich they would like – if they pay for the school lunch program. If this is not the typical procedure, then students and their parents need to be informed that a bag lunch must be packed for the field trip. The advisor should send an email (one to two days prior to the trip) to the parents of their advisees, reminding them to pack a bag lunch for their child's field trip. Parents are very busy in today's fast-paced society and will appreciate your thoughtful heads-up.

Step 5. Check with your principal to be sure the "phone tree" is fully operational. Students should not have their cellphones with them on a trip because parents are notified via cellphone from the "phone tree" callers about any problems and specifically when the bus will return – traffic permitting. These field trips are designed to be an educational experience – *school on the road* – not just a social experience. Cellphones detract from this experience. Should clever students try to disguise their hiding place for their phones and then take them out for use, simply pick up the cellphones and return them to the students at the end of the trip. The principal will decide on the consequence for such a blatant disregard for the rules. Usually, an in-house, afternoon detention will take place the following day to let other students know that there is a consequence for this type of behavior.

Step 6. Before you leave on a field trip, be sure teachers have instructed their students to always stay with their advisor throughout the trip. No one ever goes anywhere alone. Each advisor will wait outside of the restrooms and inside gift shops as well as chaperone their students throughout the duration of the trip. Teachers will periodically take a headcount of their advisees during the trip. The *critical* headcounts are before everyone leaves the school on the bus trip and before everyone departs from the location of the field trip.

Step 7. If the field trip is an overnight trip to a campsite, the procedures are basically the same. However, the duffle bags, suitcases, and sleeping bags must be loaded into the bottom of the bus, prior to departure. Be sure to check the area near the bus to be sure there is no camping equipment left behind. Upon arrival at the campsite, the camp instructors usually take charge of the field trip; teachers are sometimes asked to participate in scheduled activities, depending on the need for additional supervision. After the instructors have explained the basic rules of the camp, teachers and students are directed to the cabins. At this time, it is prudent for teachers to check the contents of the duffle bags and suitcases to be sure there are no "undesirable substances" and no candy or snacks of any kind. The raccoons will have a blast tearing apart everything in them to eat the treats. Raccoons are dangerous, so it is totally unwise of the students and teachers not to abide by the rules of the camp.

Step 8. Have fun on the field trip. There is nothing more exciting than learning on the road, visiting new places, and meeting new people. These field trips will probably be what students remember long after they have left school and are in the workplace.

Camp Mulberry

The traditional camp trip took place during the second week of school. I thought I would have some nervous students, but my students were eager and excited to be going to Camp Mulberry in New York. The camp was only one and a half hours from the school, so the short distance put parents and students at ease. Should anything go awry, parents could easily take a drive and pick up their child.

This was a "bonding trip," and the teachers and students were looking forward to three days in the wilderness. The curriculum was totally directed toward trust building, environmental projects, and river rafting. The students demonstrated their usual good behavior on the camping trip. They were cooperative in their trust building groups, and they built an amazing dome from tree branches. They learned how to navigate in the forest. However, the last day of the trip would prove to be quite a challenging experience.

The last day of the trip was devoted to river rafting. Each teacher was responsible for commandeering a raft and getting to the designated destination, which was three miles away. Paddling downstream with four, hearty, middle school students seemed like an easy task. We all donned life jackets, and we were ready for the adventure of our lives. The river had a good current heading downstream, and we began paddling our rubber raft. I was at the rear of the raft and kept the direction straight ahead by paddling on either side when I felt one side was weaker than the other. We were making great progress until the weather abruptly changed. The sky darkened with threatening clouds, and streaks of lighting shot out in front of us. I could not believe my eyes. The weather report had boasted of a sunny day. I was afraid that lightning would strike us at any moment.

My students and I sped up our paddling to travel as fast as we could, and in our haste we slid into a pile of rocks and got stuck. Summoning up my bravery, I stepped out of the raft onto a pile of rocks as slippery as a snake and almost toppled over. I grabbed the raft to steady myself and successfully pushed it forward into the water. My students burst into applause for my heroic efforts. Frankly, I thought for sure I would be sitting on the slippery rocks at any moment. The gods were with me!

Then I could not believe my ears.

One of the students whined, "I am so tired of paddling. I just cannot paddle anymore."

These wonderful students did not have any physical strength when they were faced with a minor crisis. Where was their adrenaline when they needed it? I knew this was a concern I would have to address later when we were back on dry land; however, discussing their lack of perseverance at this point in time would be counterproductive, given the impending situation.

I cajoled one student into paddling a few more strokes, but that was all he could muster. The other paddlers also gave lackluster effort in the paddling department. I simply could not believe I was the strongest paddler of them all! I was still very frightened because lightning continued to flash across the sky. I paddled for about an hour, with occasional help from my students. I do believe it was the cheering and encouragement from the students on shore that gave us the psychic and physical energy to complete the rafting journey. I was totally exhausted. It was a rafting trip *not* to be remembered.

Ellis Island

Field trips had an artistic, a scientific, a theatrical, or a historical connection to the curriculum. My favorite was the trip to Ellis Island, which was preceded by a unit called *The Immigrant Experience*. Students researched where their ancestors lived before they came to America. They learned how difficult the journey to America was and what life was like in the late 1800's and early 1900's once they arrived. They also interviewed their grandparents if they were still alive or their parents who could share their childhood memories. Finally, the students created a pedigree chart of their ancestors. Since family dynamics are different today, remain flexible regarding who your students choose to research. You should also be sensitive to the creation of everyone's pedigree chart.

Ancestral connections are very important because students learn more about themselves as individuals, and they develop a sense of pride and respect for their heritage. For example, one student found out that his ancestor was a horse trader and accumulated quite a fortune from his nefarious activities. The class had a good laugh when they heard about his ancestral discovery. This is usually not the typical information students discover about their ancestors. Most students make fascinating, historical connections to the time period in which their ancestors lived.

The day of the trip finally arrived. Students were divided into their advisory groups. They were instructed never to go anywhere alone. They had to stay in their advisory groups for the entire trip. Everyone boarded the bus, and a headcount was taken again. The students enjoyed watching a movie about Ellis Island during the trip to New Jersey. (It was always easier to leave from that location and avoid New York City traffic.) The trip was going quite well, and we were all pleased with the fine behavior of the students on the bus.

Upon arriving at our point of departure in New Jersey, the students disembarked from the bus and were handed tickets for the ferry ride to Ellis Island. The day was sunny and breezy. Everyone was anxious to see Ellis Island and search for their ancestors via computers. The ferry ride was great fun. Sitting on the top deck, we could see the Statue of Liberty, the New York City skyline, and Ellis Island. Of course, I wore my red, French beret for the trip to celebrate my country of origin, France. The students were totally into the ferry ride, socializing with their friends and observing the fantastic views from the upper deck.

After disembarking from the ferry, the students were divided into their advisory groups. We began the tour of the entire building. Students learned what tests immigrants had to pass in order to be admitted to America; they also viewed the baggage room and observed the clothing the immigrants wore. The students drew pictures of the infirmary and calculated how many people came from Europe and other countries. Then students traced their ancestry using computers and looked at the Wall of Honor to see if their relatives had contributed money to the renovated Ellis Island. We ate lunch, and then the students were told to get in line for the ferry back to the New Jersey shore.

Now here is the glitch! All the students and teachers were waiting in the line to which I had directed them for the ferry. However, I had directed the students to get in the wrong line – the line for the ferry back to New York City. The other teachers were not aware of my mistake, and we all boarded the ferry for New York City. Remember our bus was waiting for us at the New Jersey shore. I was enjoying the view from the upper deck when all of a sudden the Statue of Liberty loomed in the distance! At that moment, I realized my error. I was shocked, scared, and needed to think quickly about how to get 55 students back to the New Jersey shore. I immediately descended the stairs and spoke to the captain of the ferry, explaining what had happened. He was kind enough to let us stay aboard the ferry and *not* get off at the New York City shore. All teachers took a command post to stop all students from getting off the ferry at Battery Park in New York City. Then the captain took us to the New Jersey shore. Disaster was averted! However, the joke, which lasted a decade, was, "Mrs. R, so where is the New Jersey shore?"

Broadway Trip, New York City

Students looked forward to the yearly trip to New York City to see a Broadway musical. There was either a strong or loose connection to the curriculum. I remember seeing *The Lion King* three years in a row. The musical has the popular theme of good versus evil and is well suited to middle school students. It is always a hit with students because the musical scores are so captivating.

Newsies, the most recent Broadway musical, had a definite connection to the history curriculum because students learned what children's lives were like in America at the turn of the twentieth century. The musical was an amazing tribute to the tenacity of the young immigrants in the face of poverty and diversity; the dancing was fast paced and visually mesmerizing.

Overall, the class that we were chaperoning on the Broadway trip had good manners. However, proper theater behavior became an area of significant concern. The students were well behaved on the bus, even when the movie DVD did not work. They entertained themselves talking to one another, viewing the New York City scenery, and eating their lunches. Everything was going quite well, given that the trip took two hours to get into New York City from Connecticut. Students were instructed to get off the bus and find their advisory groups. Advisors handed out the tickets, just before we entered the theater. No tickets were lost.

Fortunately, the block of tickets, which the class dean purchased, kept the students and teachers in the same location of the theater. However, due to the frenetic process of getting all students seated on time, some students managed to change their seats in order to sit next to their friends. Friends are the *crazy glue of life* in middle school. Once the musical had begun, it was not possible to reseat the students. Since the advisors were strategically placed within the block of seats, the students were actually safe and could be monitored throughout the musical.

The protocol for attending a performance at theaters in New York City requires no talking once the show has begun. This is a novel phenomenon for middle school students. They talk nonstop and have a difficult time understanding that this behavior is not acceptable at a theater. Shushing and tapping the offenders on the shoulders finally quieted down the "talkers," and they enjoyed the show. Gentle persuasion worked on this class. There is no substitute for well brought up children in today's society; their parents believed in taking the time to teach their children good manners. Politeness never goes out of style. Should a student or group of students choose to misbehave continuously during a performance, the names of those students should be reported to the principal. These students should receive a detention for their disrespectful behavior.

Intermission was a time to be ever vigilant. Students had to be chaperoned by teachers to the men's and women's restrooms, and the remaining teachers stood near the concession stands to be sure that no one was lost in the crowd. Beverages and candy were the usually exorbitant prices, but students have an insatiable thirst for water and soda as well as for Twizzlers and boxed candy of any kind. Once the lights flickered, everyone hurried back to their seats for the second half of the musical.

Once the amazing musical was over, students were told not to leave their seats until the crowd of theatergoers had departed.

The class dean reiterated that students must remain in their advisory groups, so their advisor could get an accurate head count. The students cooperated and stayed in their advisory groups; then everyone left the theater to find the bus, which was parked one street away. To protect students from the busy traffic, teachers walked with their advisees and then became "crossing guards." This procedure was used, so teachers could be certain that their advisees were safe as they crossed the city street. Fortunately, all students arrived at the bus location, and the head count was perfect, allowing us to begin our departure. The bus ride home was pleasant because the students were tired and most fell asleep. After a two-hour bus ride home, it was a welcomed sight to view their parents eagerly awaiting their children's arrival. The parents thanked the teachers for taking their children to a Broadway musical. What a delight to have such a grateful and respectful parent body.

CHAPTER 5
PARENTS' NIGHT

The apple doesn't fall far from the tree.
–Proverb

You might wonder why Parents' Night is so important during an academic school year. Parents' Night is often strategically scheduled in early October when few grades have been given, and the focus is on meeting and greeting the parents. This evening is a not-to-be-missed opportunity to give parents an overview of your curriculum, your homework and grading policy, and the role of the advisor in middle school. You should provide paper copies of your syllabus and expectations but wait to give handouts until *after* your evening speech. Otherwise, parents will be reading the handouts rather than listening to your explanation of the expectations for your class this year. In addition, with a paper copy there will be no miscommunication should a parent be too tired to absorb the essence of your speech that evening. Finally, request that parents return a signed copy of the expectations sheet.

What is the role of the advisor? In most middle schools, a teacher also has the role of advisor and supervises at least ten advisees. The advisor is the link between the school and the parents. During Parents' Night, be sure to shake hands and welcome the parents of your advisees, making it crystal clear that your school email is the best way to communicate a concern regarding their child. You should plan on returning that email within 24 hours, so that an issue can be discussed as soon as possible. If a student is having difficulty in a particular subject area, the advisor can gather information from another teacher to try to understand where the problem lies. Often the academic problem can be identified and solved by informing both the student and the parents that after-school help is available; be sure to emphasize that taking advantage of that resource early on usually results in a successful outcome.

If the academic problem seems to be more complicated, and the student will need more support than after-school help, ask your principal or guidance counselor to find a date and time when the student, the parents, and you, the advisor, can meet to discuss the magnitude of the problem. Sometimes the student does not know how to study the academic material; suggesting a study skills tutor is often a very valuable resource that will help the student in all subject areas. The goal is to formulate a plan and get the student back on track.

The role of the advisor spans the gamut from an academic coach to an emotionally supportive coach. Students are more successful during their middle school years if they have an advisor who is troubleshooting and supporting them during those years. Middle school is frenetic enough with the emotional, social, and academic ups and downs; therefore, the advisory system is invaluable. The most important outcome is that the student feels valued as a person; learns from the difficulty he or she has faced; and forges forward with a positive outlook in the learning process. Learning is a life-long process, and it is vital that students learn to solve problems in a logical way, not shove them under the rug; with the support of the advisor, the guidance counselor, and the principal, students can learn to approach problems in a solid, sensible way, which will help them throughout their future lives.

Documentation. I cannot stress enough the importance of documentation in today's society. Teachers should keep a communication log for their advisees. This log should include not only communication with a parent but also with the student, the guidance counselor, and the administration. If any academic, athletic, or emotional problem arises, and a conference is called to discuss a problem with an advisee, you will have specific documentation from various sources to verify your information about an advisee. This documentation is crucial to having an intelligent discussion about a problem and to finding a strategy that will help a student. Parents who are asked to come to the school for a conference about their child will be expecting that you, the advisor, have thorough knowledge of their child's progress to date or lack thereof. Documentation shows your professionalism, compassion, and concern for an advisee. Your principal will be pleased that you have gathered the necessary information about an advisee to discuss a situation and create strategies in a scheduled meeting.

Most Parents' Nights result in a pleasant, social occasion. The parents are eager to take a look at you and vice versa. The principal usually gives a short speech welcoming the parents and introducing the teachers in the auditorium; then parents follow their child's schedule to the various classrooms to learn about the curriculum in each subject area. I can vividly remember one evening that was going absolutely as planned. I gave my overview of the curriculum and showed the parents which books students would be using that year. I explained the advisory system, my class expectations, and the consequences for not adhering to the script. There was a congenial, lively atmosphere in the classroom. As the parents were leaving the classroom, they thanked me for my speech and shook my hand stating that they were looking forward to an exciting year. They were also very impressed with the focus on analytical writing and critical reading. This was the last class of the evening; however, as the last couple was leaving the classroom, a father said something that was inappropriate and condescending.

As he and his wife were leaving, he rudely inquired, "I hope your teaching for the rest of the year will be as lively as your presentation this evening."

I politely replied, "Absolutely!"

Frankly, I was taken aback by his rudeness, but I kept my composure and smiled. I had never in all my years of teaching encountered such a disrespectful parent on Parents' Night.

What I really wanted to say was, "I hope you can keep pace!"

Knowing that this response would not bode well for the future, I believe my first response was the prudent one. Believe it or not, the child of that parent was a respectful, diligent child who excelled in the writing process that year. It is important to remember that as teachers we are in the profession to teach students – not their parents.

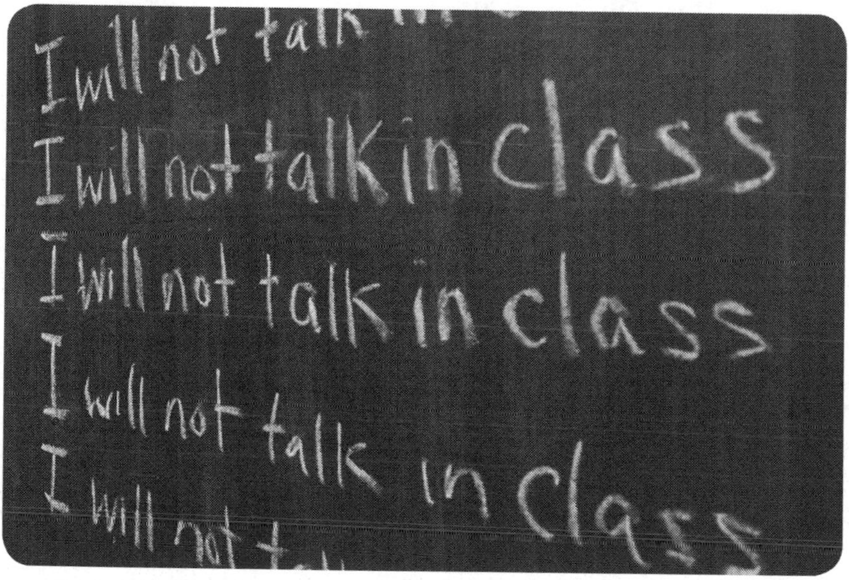
I will not talk
I will not talk in class
I will not talk in class
I will not talk in class
I will not

CHAPTER 6

DISCIPLINE

With self-discipline most anything is possible.
–Theodore Roosevelt

Unfortunately, Discipline 101 is not taught in college, and if it were, the reality of disciplining a class is very different from the college classroom version. In order for students to learn in a classroom, teachers must have excellent, classroom-management strategies. Students cannot process information effectively in a chaotic environment, especially those students who have learning issues. It is imperative that students who have difficulty with the learning process are provided with a structured, organized, quiet environment in which to understand the information in a lesson.

From day one of the academic year, students need to know that you are in charge.

There are three basic rules that will keep your classroom orderly. Explain these rules to your students on the first day of school and send a copy of the rules home to their parents with a return signature requested. That way everyone will be aware of the rules of the classroom at the beginning of the school year.

Classroom Rules

Rule One. Raise your hand to speak. No shout outs. School is not a rock concert!

Rule Two. Arrive on time for class with your books, notebooks, and computer.

Rule Three. Respect your teacher's right to teach and your classmates' right to learn.

What are the consequences for breaking classroom rules?

A student should be given a warning for the first infraction of a rule. The second time a student breaks a rule, a conversation with the student after class is necessary to find out why this misbehavior is happening again. These discussions often reveal what is really bothering the student, and together you and the student can create a plan to deter future misbehavior. It can be as simple as your looking directly at a student and giving a signal like tapping your book twice as a reminder to stop. Usually, a student would rather notice your signal or warning than continue misbehaving and suffer the consequences. However, the third time a student chooses to break a rule, the student needs to serve a detention after school. The teacher should send an email to the parents informing them why their child will be serving a detention; the parents should also be informed of the date and time of the detention, so they can make plans to pick up their child after the detention has been served. Hopefully, these detentions will not become a repeat performance, and a student will choose to obey the rules of the classroom in the future.

Middle school students will try to challenge your authority daily in the classroom. One of the clever ploys students will use to endear themselves to you will be to ask you to be their Best Friends Forever (BFF). *Tell them emphatically you do have friends – just not student friends.* Emphasize that their peers are their friends. You are their teacher, and that is a very different role. This message must resonate loud and clear; you are their teacher – not their friend.

Students in middle school like to find noises on the computer to interrupt the class. One classic noise is a computer-generated "fart machine." Students find this very funny and love to disrupt the class with this prank. It may be difficult to find the culprit because of the quick change of the computer screen at which students are so adept, but just check the history on everyone's screen. You will find the guilty party quickly. Be sure that individual is serving a detention that day. This will put an end to future pranks of this nature.

Sometimes there are disciplinary situations that become necessary to enlist other members of your faculty. Be sure to know who the go-to person is at your school. Usually, a dean is the designated person for serious infractions in the classroom. However, before you do so, you should try a few disciplinary techniques to reverse bad behavior. I would try the *time out* in the hall and a short talk to find out why a student feels the need to misbehave in the classroom. For most students, this social isolation usually needs to happen only once. If you find a student is having too many trips to the hall without any improvement in his or her behavior, it is time to send an email or make a phone call home.

It is always wise to start the conversation with an inquiry such as, "Jason has had some trouble getting his work done in class lately. Is anything unusual happening at home that I should know about?"

Believe it or not, the loss of a dog, an anticipated move, or an ill relative can wreak havoc on the emotional state of a child. This stress can directly impact a student's behavior in a classroom. Finding the underlying cause of the problem will help the student feel better and get back to enjoying the learning process once again.

Parents will be pleased that you have reached out to inform them that their child's performance has been plummeting in your class. There is nothing more important for most parents than to be informed about a problem and to have your support solving the issue. Parents want to be partners in their child's development. Middle school is a very difficult time in a child's life because middle school marks the beginning of puberty. Students and their parents struggle to cope with the fluctuating emotional and physical changes that are taking place during adolescence. Striking a balance in the lives of children, their parents, and the school requires that everyone is working in tandem for the best possible outcome, especially when problems occur. By collaborating with the teacher and being supportive of the educational goals, parents will gain a valuable support system.

If a student becomes seriously disruptive so that other students cannot learn, it is time to send that student to the dean of discipline or the assistant principal. Most schools have a number of infractions that are documented, and when a significant number of infractions have accrued, a parent is eventually requested to come to the school for a meeting with the principal, the advisor, and the teacher. Sometimes a student is asked to be part of the meeting, after the situation has been discussed and a plan of action has been outlined. That way everyone is on the same page regarding how to solve the problem.

There are several ways to help a struggling student. Most disciplinary infractions have an underlying cause, and it is often academic in nature. If a student is performing poorly in a specific class, the propensity to misbehave seems to escalate. Suggest that a student seek extra help after school or during a study hall to gain a stronger understanding of the material. Once a student has a solid grasp of the subject, he or she will feel more confident about the learning process, thus eliminating a great deal of stress. Consequently, the inclination to misbehave will often cease to be an issue. However, if after-school help does not work, hiring a private tutor for a period of time may help a student to learn the study skills necessary for success as well as gain a thorough understanding of the material.

Sometimes a disciplinary issue goes deeper than what appears on the surface. If a child has emotional issues, the principal may suggest counseling – either from a guidance counselor or from a therapist. Once the underlying issue is identified and the appropriate resources are employed to solve the problem, a student's performance usually improves along with proper, classroom behavior. Every student has the right to learn in a classroom, and no child has the right to disrupt the learning process. Since students spend a limited number of years in school, they deserve an environment that fosters the joy of discovery and a love of learning.

Middle school is a very challenging time in a student's life. Most children sail through this period, but some children find these middle school years quite turbulent. It is a time when students and their parents are trying to find a balance in their lives.

I can remember one incident that required instant disciplinary action. I was asked to come into the hallway for a brief meeting with the principal and other teachers because there was some important information about an imminent fire drill that had to be shared immediately. After carefully listening to the new instructions, I began walking toward my classroom. Before I opened the door, I heard loud hip-hop music, so I peered through the small window on the classroom door. I saw that students were gathered around in a circle, clapping their hands to the beat of the music for a student located in the center of the circle. This student was break dancing and spinning on his head! He was very adept at dancing and was enjoying the admiration of his classmates. I could not believe what I was viewing. Only five minutes out of the classroom, and my students were out of their seats having a dance party!

I immediately took charge and firmly questioned, "What is going on?"

The students were shocked that I was back in the classroom so quickly. Their total silence and surprised faces were a testimony that they should not have been dancing in my classroom. One student had the good sense to stop the music, and the students returned to their seats. I reprimanded the students about their poor judgment regarding this incident. Since all the students in the class were guilty, I kept the class in my room for recess. No one was allowed to talk for the entire recess period. Snacks were delivered to the classroom, so I would not have any parents emailing me about their children missing their nutritional snacks during recess. It is important to let students know that there are consequences for their actions, and the more immediate the consequence, the more effective the discipline.

CHAPTER 7
EXCUSES

I never knew a man who was good at making
excuses who was good at anything else.
–Benjamin Franklin

Excuses seem to be the hallmark of middle school students. The mere thought of escaping class for a few minutes to chat with their friends or creating an excuse for uncompleted homework gives them a temporary feeling of freedom and power. This *illusory power* is fleeting and has serious consequences. Little do students realize that missing class for even a short period of time creates missing links and sometimes gaps in information that will later be on tests and essays. Teachers need to be vigilant for the chronically, social "hall walkers," the "perpetually ill" students, and the "potentially dishonest Internet frauds," all of whom have as their *modus operandi* – deceit for personal gain – however short-lived that may be. It is not an easy task to detect the excuses that students have mastered over the years, but by learning a few of their typical ploys, you will be on the alert and can nip potential problems in the bud. The following examples of student excuses will give you the necessary information to put your radar on high alert for phony excuses and potential plagiarism.

What are the typical excuses students use to leave class?

Students are *masters* at creating excuses in order to avoid paying attention during class. Their acting ability at feigning sickness or desperately needing to retrieve a book or homework assignment from their locker is often Oscar worthy, so be aware of their incredible talent for deceit at a young age. Socializing with their peers is of utmost importance to middle school students, so be aware of any social activity that occurs in the hallways. Positioning yourself at the back of the room and walking around the room, so you can see who might be outside your classroom via the door window is an excellent way to view any potential socialization that is about to occur.

The following situations are a few classic examples of excuses that students often use to leave the classroom:

1. Beware of a student who *always* asks to go to the bathroom after lunch. This is usually a social event. Meeting one's friends to chat in the bathroom is a top priority. Gossiping about what went on during morning classes and during lunch is more exciting than class instruction.

2. Use a bathroom sign-out sheet for those students who use the bathroom during your class. You will have a record of the time out, the time returned, and the frequency of use. Should any problems arise, you will have a record of bathroom departures and returns.

3. Watch the student's eyes for contact with friends in the hallway. Eye contact with a friend is a signal for a sudden urge to use the facilities. (Remember socializing with one's friends is the cornerstone of a middle school student's existence.)

   "I left my homework in my locker" is a common response. This is not absentmindedness but another opportunity to connect with other "hall walkers," a student's friends.

   Should a student who is retrieving a book or homework assignment from his or her locker not return to the classroom in a few minutes, open your door and ask, "What is taking so long for you to get what you need in your locker?"

A student, who is most likely socializing with a friend, will be caught by surprise. Usually, a student will offer an apology for a wrongdoing. If this occurs, accept the apology but also issue a strong warning against a future infraction of the rules. However, should this misbehavior occur again, stronger disciplinary action would be necessary such as an after-school detention.

4. Be wary of the classic stomachache. A student who is unprepared for class often pretends to have a stomachache and asks to see the school nurse. Allow the student to go to the school nurse; however, remind the student to ask for an explanatory note with the time of departure. This time-sensitive note will dissuade the student from wandering the halls. (Also, before the student leaves your classroom, alert the school nurse via a phone call that the student is *en route* to the office.)

5. There is one situation in which you should *always* agree to a student's request to see the school nurse. When a student states that he or she is really sick and is about to vomit, immediately give the student permission to run to the bathroom. Upon the student's return to the classroom, tell the student to go to the nurse's office; you do not want the class to be further exposed to a possible, contagious germ. *Never* delay in granting this kind of request!

What deceitful excuses do students use for a late submission of an essay or a project?

1. "My computer is broken."
2. "I lost my essay when my computer shut down."
3. "We do not have ink for the printer at home."

Make it crystal clear that printing essays or projects is not done during class unless there has been a *printing emergency* at home. As clear and direct as that might seem, there will be a myriad of excuses why an assignment is not ready for submission when class begins.

These are three foolproof rules for students to learn, so assignments will be submitted on time:

1. Save the document on a flash drive and print it at school before class.
2. Save the document as an attachment to an email and send the email to your email account. Print the document at school before class.
3. Save the document in Word and send it to your teacher's email. You will not be popular with your teacher using this approach. Use this approach sparingly.

Computers are essential for students to do their homework. However, they need to realize that they are not writing their assignments with a pen or a pencil, and they must check the functionality of their computers and printers periodically. It is imperative that students learn to save their typed assignments often in order to avoid printing problems. Submitting assignments on time is a student responsibility. If students follow the aforementioned procedures and submit their assignments in a timely manner, they will learn invaluable time management skills, thus laying a foundation for their high school years.

What can you do to prevent computer problems and weed out plagiarism?

Electronic submissions for essays are the current trend. Students who may have computer problems at home can always use a school computer to complete the essay. It may be inconvenient to stay after school, but it will keep a student current with assignments. It will also give the student and the parents time to address the malfunctioning computer problem at home. Ironically, the "malfunctioning" sometimes can be procrastination on the student's part because the assignment was never completed in the first place; therefore, this option of completing an assignment on a school computer will eliminate all excuses. This method of electronic submission allows teachers to give timely feedback and to be vigilant for plagiarism. The most useful computer tools to detect plagiarism are *Turn It In* and *Google Docs*.

CHAPTER 8

CONFERENCES

Once you meet the parents of your advisees, you will understand a great deal about your advisees. The roots of the parent and child relationship begin at home. Parents are the child's first teachers. Some parents are very good at this role, and others really are not prepared for parenting. They will be too busy advancing their own careers to do much substantial parenting. You will recognize those parents instantly because they will want you to do their parenting as well as your teaching. The conversation usually sounds like the following scenario:

"You are so much better at talking about the importance of doing daily homework than I am," stated Ms. Parent.

"I can talk to your child about being diligent regarding daily assignments, but you are the one at home who needs to supervise the homework. You do not have to do the work – just oversee your child's homework in each subject every night. Then put a check mark in your child's daily planner for completed work," replied Ms. R.

Remember parents are partners in their child's school experience. You can be the guiding light and pedagogue during the day at school, but parents need to do their part for the academic success of their child.

Always be professional regarding your role as an educator. Be sensitive to the needs of each student, but know that there is an invisible line that separates you from the student. You are not the student's friend. You are not the student's BFF. You are not the student's surrogate parent, either. Excellent schools focus on the academic, athletic, and artistic life of the child; schools should also create an atmosphere where each child feels physically safe and emotionally comfortable at school. Since parents are very busy today, it is essential that you gain their support. Parent conferences are an excellent time to garner their support.

Conferences are an important way to assess the progress of your students. The most effective way for parents to learn about their child's progress is during the fall conference, which usually takes place in early November. Advisors should start collecting quizzes, tests, and projects from their advisees each week, beginning the first week of school. Create folders for each of your advisees and place the aforementioned papers in those folders; keep the folders in a safe, plastic box for easy reference and retrieval for future conferences.

Inform your advisees that during advisee periods they will be creating goals for each trimester. Ask your advisees to write a goal for each academic subject. Never accept the following as a goal: "I want an A in every subject." Remind your advisees that they must write realistic and attainable goals, given their aptitude and interest in a particular subject. Explain that *how* they reach a specific goal is essential; therefore, students need to list a strategy for each goal they wish to accomplish. For example, a student might write a strategy to seek after-school help in biology. This is a specific strategy that will help a student to reach a future goal. These goals will be the focus of your discussions with their parents during conferences.

When conference time is approaching, you need to have a one-on-one practice session (pre-conference) with each of your advisees. As you look over the representative work for the trimester, if you sense that a student has only put in the good tests, quizzes, and projects, ask him or her to find "the good, the bad, and the ugly work" from the trimester. Students often try to hide their poor scores, which inevitably show up on their report card. Explain to each advisee that conference time is a time to review what a student has done well and a time to find where a student needs to improve moving forward. Discuss the goals that your advisees set for themselves in the fall and ask if they have reached those goals. If not, then question them to ascertain if they have gone for extra help in subjects that they have found difficult. Suggest that they should seek extra help in the future, even if they have not done so this past trimester.

Then establish new goals with your advisees, with a plan of action, for the next trimester. This plan should include the following: finding a quiet place to study without texting, seeking extra help when necessary, keeping current with homework assignments, taking more thorough notes, and packing one's backpack with books and completed homework every night in preparation for the next day of school. I would explain this "plan of action" to the student's parents during the conference. Encourage parents to help their child to accomplish these goals by checking that homework has been done in a timely manner and their child's backpack is packed with the appropriate books, computer, notebooks, and homework every night. In addition, if a student is truly struggling, even after going for extra help in a particular subject, suggest that parents provide a tutor for a period of time until the child has a solid grasp of the material.

Unfortunately, some parents act like Attila the Hun at conferences. They have long forgotten what it is like to be a teenager, struggling to achieve success in all subjects, while using their maximum potential. Conferences today often require a student's presence. Usually, a student presents and discusses a trimester's work in all subjects with accompanying quizzes, tests and projects, to his parents with the assistance of the advisor. If you should encounter a compassionless parent, remember you are the student's advocate. Take charge of the conference by focusing on the good academic results to date; then strategize how a student can do better work in other subjects for the next trimester. Never let a student be browbeaten by a parent during a conference. If a student is really struggling, suggest that the student seek extra help, learn better study skills, and/or get a tutor for a particularly difficult subject. Collaborate with the student and the parents to devise a plan with specific guidelines and daily support, so the student can begin to acquire the necessary knowledge in a particular subject. Once a student begins to experience academic accomplishments again, his or her level of confidence will grow exponentially, and success will follow. Students who learn how to advocate for themselves by seeking extra, academic support in middle school will be learning one of the most valuable lessons for their future, academic years.

Occasionally, you may encounter parents who do not respect the scheduled time for their child's conference and continue to talk beyond their allotted time slot. Handling this situation requires tactful strategies. First, always be aware of the time when a conference should begin and end. You should have a list of parents' names and their scheduled, conference times next to you. Always face the clock in your room or wear a watch, so you are aware of the passage of time for each scheduled conference. It is unfair to have two or three parents wait an extra twenty to thirty minutes in the hallway for their child's conference because you allowed one parent to monopolize your time. You must take control of the scheduled conferences, so all parents feel respected and have the appropriate amount of time to discuss their child's progress.

If it appears that a conference will be going into overtime, politely and firmly say, "We only have five more minutes left for this conference. Is there one, final topic you would like to discuss?" Most parents will understand your request and discuss one last issue. However, some parents simply do not care about the time frame and will continue talking as if they have unlimited access to your time during their conference.

You will have to use the second strategy on these parents. Interrupt parents in the middle of a sentence if they do not let you get a word in the conversation and state, "I am sorry, but we have gone beyond the scheduled conference time today. If you would like to set up another appointment, please check your schedule and email me, so we can meet again at a mutually convenient time." Most parents understand this logical approach to discussing further concerns that they may have about their child.

Unfortunately, there are always the parents who just keep talking and sit there as if they were glued to the chair, so you will have to use this third strategy. You must interrupt them by asserting, "I have several other parents who are scheduled for conferences, and they have been patiently waiting in the hallway. Thank you for coming to today's conference. Should you wish to discuss any other concerns about your child, please check your schedule and email me, so we can meet again at a mutually convenient time."

As you say these words, stand up and slowly walk to the door in your classroom. Once you have opened the door, the parents should be following you.

Always shake hands with the students' parents and thank them for coming to the conference. Most parents are polite and respectful regarding the scheduled, conference time for their child. Conferences are an essential part of the learning process because it is a time when the child, the parents, and the teacher can review a trimester's work, analyze what is working and what needs improvement, and establish new goals and strategies for future trimesters. These conferences are great markers in a school year for evaluation and reflection. Those students and parents who come to a conference with a positive attitude leave with information about their child's performance and with a plan for moving forward for the rest of the school year.

Chapter 9

Cellphones

Cellphones have become a controversial issue in schools today. Every school has a different stance on the issue. Some schools have tried to ban cellphones completely; however, after trying to enforce this policy, they realized that a daily cellphone search was completely unrealistic and a waste of time. Therefore, policies on cellphones have become more flexible in most schools with certain restrictions on when and where students may use them.

Students today have grown up in a technological world. They have had access to computers, cellphones, email, and the Internet from birth. They are digitally savvy and rely on their cellphones for communication in society. It is a reality that most students in school have a cellphone today. Students are comfortable with technology and view it as an integral part of their lives.

Some schools have instituted a policy that allows cellphones to be used during non-instructional periods such as between classes and at lunch. In addition, cellphones may also be used in classes as learning tools. Teachers who have incorporated cellphones in the classroom feel that students have become more actively engaged in the learning process.

How are cellphones used in the classroom? Cellphones have been used for small group research races. The website polleverywhere. com allows teachers to ask a question, and then students text their answers to a specific number that the teacher gives them.

The website collects the data and creates a graph from their responses. This information in the graph allows students to discuss the results in a timely manner. This use of cellphones creates a learning environment that is exciting and relevant.

Another use of cellphones is in language classes. Students can learn how to pronounce words and then speak to each other in French, Spanish, and many other languages. Auditory learning, using cellphones, is actively engaging the students' minds and social skills.

Many teachers now use Dropbox where they can post reading assignments, links to the Internet, or changes in homework assignments on the school website. This method has proved to be very efficient for teachers because students can access Dropbox from their cellphones. Cellphone applications can be used in many other disciplines such as math, science, English, history, and the arts to enhance each respective curriculum.

There are additional pros regarding the use of cellphones in the classroom:

1. **Emergency Contact**. Parents need to be able to contact their child if an emergency occurred. Sometimes the protocol of going through the main office and locating a child in a classroom delays an immediate contact with their child, which can exacerbate an already critical situation. A cellphone is a direct link with their child in an emergency.
2. **Security**. Parents who work need to be in contact with their child for a pick-up point or a change in time. Students who have cellphones also can have immediate access to 911, a hospital, or a relative if needed.
3. **Academic Uses**. There are several ways that cellphones can be academically useful. Cellphones can be used as basic or scientific calculators. Cameras on cellphones can be used to take photos of specific historical landmarks or statues – later to be part of a class presentation. Students who are

late for their next class can use their cellphones to take a snapshot of the notes on the board. This is especially helpful for a student with a visual learning disability. In addition, students can use a schedule on cellphones to enter dates for upcoming tests as well as access academic websites for projects. When used appropriately, cellphones enhance the learning environment.

Unfortunately, there are some cons connected with the use of cellphones at school:

1. **Texting**. Students who have access to their cellphones in class are often tempted to text their friends rather than focus on the lesson. Students are very adept at texting without looking at the keyboard, and they can send and receive messages faster than the speed of a teacher's glance.
2. **Ringing**. Even a phone that is vibrating or melodiously ringing can be a distraction, thus preventing students from fully concentrating during class. Oftentimes, these cellphones can be found in students' backpacks, boots, or jackets; no matter where they are located, the sounds emanating from the cellphones disrupt the class. Not only is this auditory intrusion disrespectful to the teacher, it is also lost time for class instruction.
3. **Cheating**. Cellphones have been used in three ways to cheat on a test. First, a student can use the Internet to find answers while taking a test. Second, one student can text another student for an answer during a test in the classroom or text an accomplice to meet in the bathroom for information. Third, a student can photograph information from a book and then access the information while taking a test. It is shocking that cheating is so rampant in schools today. Some students need to re-discover their moral compass. Perhaps

if they are caught cheating, the consequence will be stiff enough to make them honest citizens in the future.

4. **Illegal Uses**. Cellphones in the hands of wayward students can create major problems for schools and communities. Some students have no qualms of conscience calling in a bomb threat simply as a prank to get out of classes. Other students could use their cellphones to sell drugs or engage in thievery. Unguarded laptops have been stolen at schools. These kinds of behavior are not the norm, but they do happen on school grounds.

What can teachers do to encourage the appropriate use of cellphones in school?

Teachers need to be the guardians of cellphone use in their school. When students are engaged in meaningful work in a classroom, cellphones serve a solid, academic purpose. However, if you notice a group of students laughing at a photo on a cellphone, and the conversation surrounding the photo has the intent to bully another student, it is your duty to report the students involved in the incident. Confiscate the cellphone and report the situation immediately to your principal. Social harassment is never an appropriate use of cellphones.

If you observe potential criminal activity such as students using their cellphones to sell drugs or to rob someone, alert the principal at once. Do not put yourself in danger of being harmed. Unnoticeably, walk away from the scene of the potential crime and either call the office from your classroom phone or from your cellphone to report the nefarious activity on school property. Overall, the benefits of using cellphones in school far outweigh the negative effects. Allowing students to carry a cellphone to school creates a safe connection between students and their parents. Using cellphones for academic purposes allows technology to be an integral part of the learning process in schools today.

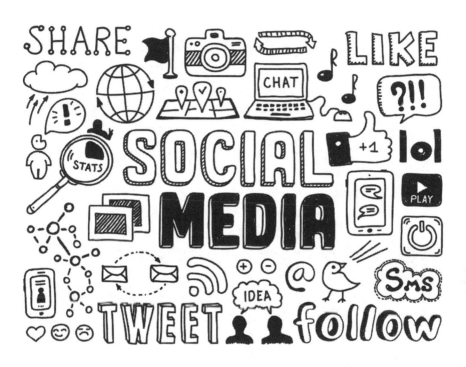

CHAPTER 10

FACEBOOK

Facebook is a social networking site used by over one billion people. The site allows people to interact virtually via email, instant messaging, and blog-like posts. Students, adults, schools, businesses, non-profit organizations, and religious houses of worship have created Facebook accounts to share and update information. Facebook is a powerful means of communication that connects people globally.

Despite the remarkable virtual connections that Facebook offers, there are a few concerns that I would like to mention regarding how students use the site. When students are using their Facebook accounts, they tend to lose track of how much time they are spending on this site. Minutes can lapse into hours, and students are unaware of how much time has been spent socializing with one's friends. Due to the social nature of the site, some students have become addicted to Facebook and spend an inordinate amount of time on it, leaving very little quality time to do their homework. Therefore, parents need to set parameters for their children, limiting the time their children are allowed to spend on Facebook daily.

Another concern is the concept of friends on Facebook. Students state that they have over one hundred friends on the site. The reality is that most of these friends are virtual friends. In the real world, most students have a few close friends and several additional friends. When students spend too much time on Facebook with their virtual friends, they do not engage in healthy activities like sports or listening to music with their real friends.

It is essential to socialize with one's friends to develop communication skills. By only socializing virtually, students never learn the appropriate communication skills they will need during their academic school years as well as during their working years.

Face-to-face communication is very different from virtual communication. When students talk to one another, they learn to read people's emotions from the conversation; this kind of feedback from someone's facial expressions is invaluable to have an in-depth conversation with another person. These essential skills should be developed when students are in the formative stages of their academic development, so they will be prepared for the real world as they move into adulthood.

My final concern involves the numerous incidents of bullying that happen on Facebook. Due to the apparent *invisible* nature of the site, a bully can surreptitiously hide behind the virtual communication on Facebook. Statements made on this site are often more hurtful because the victim does not know who is actually saying these mean words. If these negative words are repeated enough times, the victim can become depressed and even suicidal. As an educator, if you are aware of this destructive behavior happening on school grounds using Facebook, it is incumbent on you to confront the bully, confiscate the computer, and print the evidence. Bring your findings and the student's computer to the principal, so the bully can be properly punished. It is unfortunate that some students choose to use Facebook in a socially unacceptable and destructive manner.

Facebook can be a blessing or a bane to a teacher's existence. I will relate how dangerous Facebook can be. I had a fake Facebook account that I did *not* create. It took years to resolve the issue. Many school districts monitor teachers' Facebook accounts for inappropriate behavior. You could lose your job and your teacher certification if you choose to use Facebook improperly. Be careful. *Never "friend" a student.*

How did this happen? Someone in one of my classes created a fake Facebook account by taking a photo of me with an angry face, when I was criticizing a student for not focusing in class. Now I had a fake Facebook account. I had been unaware that I even had a fake Facebook account until a sensible student showed me "my account" on his cellphone. To my surprise, when the student showed me the imposter account, I had numerous connections with positive statements from good students. As reassuring as this was, I did not want an imposter account managed by a student who obviously had a problem with me.

Clearly, it was time to analyze who might have created this fake Facebook account. I thought I had a fairly good idea who might have been bold enough to do so. A new student to the school was transferred out of my class to the next grade level early in the school year, due to a mistake in placement. Upon confronting this student in the hallway one day, he smiled sheepishly and denied any wrongdoing. Without any proof, I was powerless to accuse this student of creating an imposter Facebook account and bring him to the principal.

Then I asked my principal and a colleague to report the incident to Facebook, which they did. Supposedly, the account was to be deleted, due to the imposter nature of the account. Three years later, the account was still on Facebook.

I was very concerned and perplexed about the situation. Having a fake Facebook account in my name to which anyone could respond with whatever information they wished to portray concerned me. I had to get this account closed. Fortunately, a parent of a student in my terrific class worked at a business where someone knew how to delete a Facebook account. I was relieved when this account was finally deleted.

The Internet is an amazing invention, but if someone chooses to use it to damage your reputation, it can be devastating. Facebook is a great form of social media when used properly. Monitor the use of Facebook as much as possible, so that your identity is protected.

CHAPTER 11
BULLYING

Bullying is an unconscionable behavior that cannot be overlooked in schools. This behavior takes many forms: physical bullying, emotional bullying, and cyber bullying. The bully insists on controlling another student through physical force, verbal abuse, or Internet abuse. This behavior is detrimental to the victim; therefore, it is the teacher's job to identify the bully and bring the student to the principal's office for disciplinary action. It is now the law in many states that bullying in schools is a punishable offense. Teachers have the most direct contact with students, and they must be constant observers for bullying behavior on school grounds. Teachers are mandatory reporters of bullying incidents.

In many schools, students are taught about bullying in anti-bullying programs. There are three roles in the bullying scenario. There is the bully; there is the target or victim; and there is the bystander. The bully is exhibiting negative behavior to gain recognition from his or her classmates, who are usually too frightened to articulate their opposition. Often a bully has been bullied by someone else and is simply repeating learned behavior. The bully may be narcissistic, trying to control anxiety or cover up low self-esteem; whatever the bully's motivation may be for engaging in negative behavior, it must be stopped, and the principal must take appropriate action. Why? Every child has the right to learn in a safe environment without fear, teasing, humiliation, or assault.

Students should be taught the necessary skills to deal with bullies in a Life Skills Class. They can be taught how to speak up for one another. As difficult as it may be to stand up for another student, it is easier if students rehearse scenarios and do simulations. They can learn the appropriate, effective language to use during these simulations, so when a real-life situation occurs, they will be prepared with the most direct, prepared responses to stop a bully. Simulations have proved to be an effective method to train students to stand up to a bully, so they will not be bystanders during an incident.

Bullying is sometimes difficult to detect, but it is a teacher's job to be ever vigilant for negative behavior that clearly speaks to bullying in the classroom, in the hallways, in the locker room, in the lunchroom, and on school computers. If school computers are used for cyber bullying, a teacher needs to find evidence of the conversation on the student's computer and print out a copy of the information for the principal. This evidence must be brought to the principal immediately. Usually, a bullying incident with documented evidence results in a suspension for such a reprehensible offense.

Students who are bullied lose their sense of self, become depressed, feel like social outcasts, and sometimes contemplate or commit suicide. Cyber bullying especially needs to be monitored very carefully. Since bullies can use emails, instant messaging, Twitter, and Facebook to bully a victim, the rapidity with which an original message can be sent and resent, with additional information by other Internet users, can be devastating to the victim. Therefore, discovering the bully is essential to ascertaining the culprit and reporting this wrongdoer to the principal.

Bystanders play a significant role in the bullying process. Students who are bystanders and are brave enough to speak up during a situation when someone is being bullied often can reroute the bullying. For example, a scenario might involve a group of popular girls, where one of the girls is a bully and has decided to berate the victim for wearing an outfit that she deems to be out of style. One of the popular girls with a conscience simply has to say, "Everyone is an individual, and she has a right to choose what she likes to wear." This type of positive statement from a former bystander can usually defuse the situation, and the bully will back off. It takes a lot of courage to speak up in such a situation, but occasionally one of the popular girls may still have a moral compass.

Years ago when the Internet was not part of the school scene, bullying existed in schools. The bullying was usually among boys and was physical. For example, the larger boys in sports programs thought nothing of stuffing younger students in a large, plastic, trash barrel and laughing at their victims. Usually, a coach did not detect bullying in the locker room because he was too busy collecting sports equipment for the session. Some coaches were aware of the bullying that took place, and they ignored it. Popular opinion among coaches a quarter of a century ago was that boys needed to toughen up, and a bullying incident was all in fun. Most likely these coaches had been bullied during sports when they were young boys, and they simply endured this abusive behavior. Consequently, these coaches were simply repeating history when they ignored bullying incidents.

However, today coaches have to respond to these incidents or face the possibility of losing their jobs. They may even end up in court over an unreported, bullying incident in the locker room. Years ago the bullies were not punished, but the victims felt the emotional and physical pain many years later. Bullying in the locker room, in the classroom, in the lunchroom, or anywhere on a school campus is **never** acceptable and must be reported.

Today bullied victims have reached even higher risk situations. The power of the printed word in text messages, photos on Facebook, and other media communication on the Internet have sometimes escalated to dire situations. The students are ashamed, fearful, and depressed. Too many times there is no teacher who is willing to document bullying incidents and report the situation to the principal. The student feels helpless and hopeless, ending the abuse by committing suicide. This cycle of abuse must be stopped because bullying at its worst results in death. As a teacher, it is your responsibility to be ever vigilant for bullying situations and report them to your principal immediately.

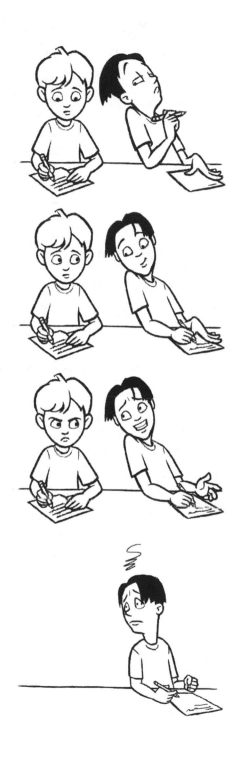

CHAPTER 12

CHEATING

**Three things cannot be long hidden:
the sun, the moon and the truth.**
–Buddha

Unfortunately, cheating is on the rise in today's schools. As a teacher, you must be vigilant when giving quizzes and tests. Students have a myriad of ways to cheat, and I will explain how they will cleverly cheat right in front of your eyes – unless you are aware of the *tricks of the trade.*

The best way to avoid cheating in your classroom is to separate desks or place two students at the far end of each table with a plastic divider between the students. If you do not have plastic dividers, then have students place a pile of books or binders on the table to separate them from other students. Tell your students that they must keep their eyes on their own quiz or test. If you see them looking at someone else's quiz or test, quietly go to their desk and pick up their test. They will receive a zero on the quiz or test, and that will automatically make their grade average plummet. Then report the cheating incident to the principal, which will most likely result in a suspension. The incident will also be part of their permanent school record. Clearly, this is not a document anyone wants on a school record. Reiterate this fact to your classes.

Today, cheating has become more sophisticated with the use of cellphones. Cellphones can be used to share information that is on a test by texting the key information to another student in between classes or during a *necessary* trip to the bathroom. Avoid allowing students to use the bathroom during a test – unless there is an emergency. Some brazen students might even try to text information during a test – if a teacher is busy correcting papers at a desk and not paying attention to the students in the classroom. How do they do that? They hide their cellphones in their pockets, boots, and even under a pile of books. That is why it is imperative that teachers walk around the classroom when giving a quiz or test. Never underestimate the old-fashioned technique of printing answers on one's hands or arms the evening before a test – only to be used surreptitiously the next day in class. Students who intend to cheat are very creative and will go to unimagined lengths to complete their *dastardly deeds*. You need to be one step ahead of the cheaters.

The incident I remember most vividly involved a student who was given an assignment to write an original poem. The poem could be free verse, so the requirements were minimal. The student in question decided to put super-minimal effort into creating his poem to fulfill the assignment. After I collected all the poems from the class, I began correcting this student's poem that evening. I recognized the professional nature of this one student's submission. I read the poem twice to be sure that I was not being overly suspicious. My next move was to Google five words of the poem. His poem appeared on the Internet! He had changed only a few words in the poem and was definitely guilty of plagiarism. I was quite shocked because this student had never cheated before.

After class the next day, I asked this student to meet me in the teacher's office to ensure privacy, so that other students could not hear our conversation. *It is very important to find a quiet place to talk about such a serious situation.* I asked him if he had used the Internet to help him to write his poem. At first, he seemed confused about the question, but when I showed him the poem he had submitted and compared it to the poem on the Internet, he confessed to plagiarizing the poem. He stated that he had trouble creating an original poem. I told him that any original, honest attempt at creating a free verse poem would have been a much wiser choice to complete this assignment.

I further explained the seriousness of this offense and that I had to report the incident to the principal. I also told him the true story about a college student who attended Brown University several years ago. This student was a senior and decided to plagiarize her history paper; the consequence was very serious for her offense because she did *not* graduate from that university. Not only had she wasted thousands of dollars of her parents' money but also had damaged her reputation by engaging in plagiarism. The consequence in my student's case was milder than I had anticipated because it was a first offense in middle school for this student; the principal issued a strong warning to the student stating that if plagiarism ever occurred again, it would be an immediate suspension. However, the student did receive a zero for the assignment, lowering his overall grade. He understood the serious nature of plagiarism and learned from his deviant behavior. I am pleased to say that this student went on to perform well in high school and graduated with honors.

CHAPTER 13

SCHOOL SAFETY

One of the most important issues in schools today is safety. For all schools, the safety issue has become a priority, due to recent school invasions throughout the country. The amount of funding that a school district spends to upgrade safety in school buildings is directly correlated to the school budget. There are several different approaches that school systems have taken to keep students, teachers, administrators, and other personnel safe. For school systems whose budgets are limited, outside doors are locked throughout the school day. After ascertaining that the person seeking entrance into the building is appropriate, an administrative assistant then answers the door and allows the visitor into the building. The visitor must sign in at the office and explain the reason for coming to the school. A pass is given to the visitor for the duration of the visit, which must be returned to the administrative assistant upon leaving the building.

Some school districts have installed surveillance cameras near the front office and throughout the school building, which run 24/7. Visitors are buzzed in, if they are deemed appropriate, and then they follow the same procedure as the aforementioned visitor who has been met at the door. In addition, controlled access to school grounds during school hours occurs at some schools, and cameras continue to record who comes on the school property after school is closed. Using surveillance technology is the most efficient and thorough safety measure that a school system can implement to create a safe environment.

What is the teacher's role in building safety? Teachers should always arrive at school at least fifteen minutes (preferably a half hour) before the students. They should be available to meet the students at the entrance of the school in the morning – if there is an assigned list of teachers to do so. Meeting and greeting students at the entrance of the school creates a safe and friendly environment. If teachers are not on duty for the morning welcome, they should be in the hallway and/or in their classrooms to supervise students in the morning. Once the students have arrived by bus or car, they should promptly go into the school. Then they need to go to their lockers, unpack their book bags, and gather the books and notebooks they need for their classes.

Teachers should always be vigilant for unfamiliar faces in the building. If you notice anyone who appears suspicious, you should walk up to the person and ask, "May I help you?" Usually, parents or interns will identify themselves immediately and explain why they are in the building. However, if an unidentified person were to give a questionable response, instantaneously call the office from your room and report that a person of dubious character is in the hallway near the classrooms. Always remain calm and professional when talking to a stranger. Never hint that you are suspicious or nervous, which could make a situation escalate. If your school has a surveillance camera, the administrative assistant can zoom in on the individual, and the principal can take control of the situation. If there is no surveillance video system, your informative phone call to the principal will be invaluable. Remember to give specific details about the location of the stranger. Then let the principal deal with the problem while you keep your students safe.

At dismissal time, teachers are usually assigned to bus duty or car pick-up locations. It is vitally important that you are at your designated location on time. Once all students have left the building, the outside door is locked. Students should be promptly directed either to the bus or to the car that will transport them home. No student should be lingering on campus after dismissal. Strict rules for entrance to and from the school building need to be enforced for everyone's safety in the school community.

Lockdowns are another preventative measure to keep students safe. Practice drills for lockdowns should take place at least three times each school year – once a trimester. Students must learn the beeping sound of a lockdown; it is different from the sound of a fire drill. Students are instructed to stay away from windows and crouch down near a wall where an intruder cannot see them. They must be absolutely silent and listen to instructions from their teacher. The teacher locks the door from the inside; the key is always part of a teacher's school key chain and should be either hooked to a belt or attached to a neck chain. Students must be further instructed that if they happen to be in the bathroom during a lockdown and hear the lockdown beep, they must run to the closest classroom. These lockdowns *must* be taken seriously.

Any student who does not follow the lockdown procedures must be sent to the principal after the practice drill. A student who does not follow lockdown rules is placing everyone in serious danger. There should be zero tolerance for disrespecting lockdown drills, and the student who has disobeyed the procedures should be disciplined with an immediate detention. Often isolating a student for a lunch detention in a classroom is effective; a dean or an advisor should explain the gravity of the student's misbehavior during that lunch detention. Usually, this in-house detention is a wake-up call to the student. Students at the middle school level treasure their lunch period with their friends, and they do not want to spend time with a teacher in a disciplinary detention. Having a one-on-one discussion about the seriousness of the lockdown drill should deter the student from further misbehavior in the future. If this behavior occurs again during another practice lockdown, then a meeting with the student's parents and the principal should be called to further discuss the refractory behavior.

Fire drills are required several times a year by law for all schools, public and independent. Students must be clearly instructed in advance as to which staircase and door to use when exiting the building. When the fire drill, screeching sound happens, they can exit the building quietly and walk to a designated location – usually a nearby sports field. The *no talking rule* must be obeyed, and time is of the essence when practicing a fire drill. The principal monitors the time it takes for the students, teachers, and administrators to evacuate the school building and then informs the students exactly how much time the evacuation took. If the time is unsatisfactory, and the students have not taken the fire drill seriously, repeated drills are essential for the safety of the students and all other personnel. It is imperative to get a quick evacuation of the building in silence, so everyone will be prepared in case of a real fire.

Interviews with the press, either with a television reporter or with a local journalist from a newspaper should only be held with the principal. It is not a teacher's role to relay facts about an incident with the aforementioned media personnel. Always defer to a principal or head of school regarding information about a situation that may have occurred at your school.

Be sure to follow the rules of the school to the letter of the law. Usually, all these rules are in a manual or online for you to read and sign off on, stating that you have read them. I would suggest that you read the manual several times to be absolutely sure you know what to do in a crisis. Also keep a copy of the basic rules for a lockdown or a fire drill close at hand – should you need to refer to them quickly in an emergency situation. Remember that the students, faculty, parents, and administration are all counting on you to know what to do to protect the safety of everyone involved. To be informed is essential and to act accordingly is expected. Keeping a cool head and a logical demeanor will help you through any situation you might face.

CHAPTER 14
COLLEAGUES

> Coming together is a beginning: keeping together
> is progress; working together is success.
> –Henry Ford

The people with whom you work are very important. You are with them for most of your workday, so cooperation and communication are essential to creating a harmonious life at school. Think of your school as your home away from home. When you attend the first faculty meeting of the year and are introduced, all eyes will be on you. Dress in a conservative, professional manner. Pants with a blouse, a skirt with a dressy jersey, or a conservative dress complemented by flats or heels will create a positive image for all female teachers. Male teachers should wear collared shirts and khakis or grey pants with brown or black shoes. No jeans or sneakers on the first day of school. *First impressions are lasting impressions.* Should the dress code for teachers become more relaxed in the spring, due to warmer weather, you may wear a more casual yet appropriate style of clothing.

Usually, a mentor is assigned to a first-year teacher to impart information about various school procedures and activities throughout the school year. For example, a mentor explains what to expect on parents' night and at conferences. A mentor also clarifies how to navigate the computer-generated, homework assignments and the grading system as well as how to communicate with difficult parents. However, should your mentor be a science teacher, who is located on the other side of the building, do not hesitate to become fast friends with a teacher in your office who can get you up to speed on the previously mentioned procedures. Do not try to go it alone. Experienced teachers who are willing to share their wisdom are worth their weight in gold. They can save you a great deal of angst and maybe even your job, especially when it comes to dealing with challenging, troublesome parents.

An experienced mentor can make your school year almost *a walk in the park*. Teaching is never going to be an easy job, but having someone who gives you a heads up about important aspects of the school, parents, the administration, and social obligations will definitely make your first year a pleasant one. Navigating the social climate of the school is more treacherous than you might imagine. A mentor can forewarn you about how to handle an angry or inquisitive parent who might show up at your doorstep without an appointment. Technically, most schools require that a parent email a teacher to set up an appointment – not just show up at any random time and day. In today's busy world, it is presumptuous and disrespectful for a parent to simply arrive at a teacher's door after school and expect to discuss a problem. Teachers do have lives outside of the classroom; therefore, appointments are essential for effective communication.

I can vividly remember one parent in particular who felt she had the right to cruise the hallways any day she chose during sports period. This period was just before students were dismissed to go home. All students were at sports, so the halls were empty except for a sports study hall in one of the classrooms for students who had injuries. She knew it was prime time to find a teacher in either a classroom or in an office to ask for *a few minutes* to discuss her daughter's progress in a particular class. Teachers were on the lookout for Ms. Stealth. Everyone knew her request for a brief update would take an hour of discussion.

Since this period of the day was extremely valuable for teachers to correct papers or prepare lessons, all teachers tried to avoid getting trapped in this scenario.

The only way to eventually handle Ms. Stealth was to preface one's remarks by saying, "I have a meeting in twenty minutes, but we can talk briefly about your daughter's progress."

As time elapsed that year, Ms. Stealth tried the same *modus operandi* with all her daughter's teachers. However, Ms. Stealth's reputation as a cunning hall walker became widely known, and all the teachers held fast to asking this parent to set up an appointment to discuss her concerns about her daughter in the future. This procedure worked very well once Ms. Stealth realized her shrewd tactics would not be acceptable protocol at this school.

However, if there is a crisis of some nature, then your classroom must be open to discuss the situation immediately. If you encounter a student who has been bullied and is crying after a sports period, do be compassionate and promptly discuss the issue. This would be a time to include the student's advisor (if available) and the school principal. If the parent arrives at your doorstep (students often use their cellphones to inform their parents about the situation), deal with the crisis at once. Students in middle school have a more difficult time maintaining their emotional equilibrium because they are going through so many emotional and physical changes at the same time. By being there for a student at a crucial time, you can listen and offer to get all the facts so that the situation does not escalate. It is the teacher's role to be available and supportive during a crisis.

Always include your principal in the process of finding out what happened and how the problem can be resolved.

CHAPTER 15
SOCIAL RESPONSIBILITY

**The task of the modern educator is not to
cut down jungles but to irrigate trees.**
–C. S. Lewis

Teaching is a full-time commitment, as all dedicated teachers will agree. Evenings and weekends are busy with lesson preparation, correcting papers, and recording grades. However, in addition to the standard, job requirements, there are several expected social responsibilities that cannot be ignored because they are an integral part of the job.

The first responsibility you will be asked to attend is Open House. At an independent school, this happens in October, and you are expected to be there. It is a time to show the prospective students what it is like to attend your school. The principal or head of school gives an overview of the school's programs and some background about the history of the school to the entire audience.

Then parents and students are divided into groups, according to grade level, for a tour of the school – led by current students who have volunteered to be guides for the day. These guides will inform prospective students and parents about a typical school day at their school, and then they will stop by your classroom to introduce you. After the introduction, it will be your turn to welcome everyone, explain your curriculum, show your textbooks, and answer any questions that the visitors might have about your course or about any part of the school day. This afternoon serves both a social and an academic purpose. You will find that it is a cordial exchange between the prospective parents, their child, the student guides, and the teachers. It is a required afternoon because October is the month in which parents begin searching for a new, independent school for their child to attend the following year.

Another significant responsibility is a teacher's presence at games. Teachers should carve out time at the end of a busy, teaching day to cheer for their students at soccer, volleyball, football, or field hockey games during the fall season. Students love to have a teacher's support at games, and in return, you will gain firsthand knowledge of their athleticism and sportsmanship. If you have to write recommendations for students who may be applying to other schools in the future, your attendance at these games will give you direct insight into their character as displayed on the field or on the court. Recommendations always have three main areas where you will be asked to give your evaluation of a student; namely, academics, athletics, and character. Therefore, attendance at athletic events is an essential requirement for being a responsible, informed, and valued teacher.

In the winter, it is always fun to go to basketball games. Again, you should show your support by cheering for your students at games. It is amazing how the adrenaline gets pumping when you get involved and start rooting for your home team. The break from correcting papers is good for the psyche. Finally, in the spring, attendance at lacrosse, baseball, or track meets is required.

In conjunction with sports is the annual homecoming event, which happens in October. *See and be seen* is very important at this event because you are demonstrating school spirit and support. It is important that your principal is aware of your attendance, so be sure to say, "Hello," with a friendly smile. Games are scheduled throughout a designated Saturday for homecoming, and the football game usually draws the largest number of spectators, especially students, faculty, and alums. It is also a time to enjoy shopping for athletic apparel with school logos or for homemade pastries at the various booths run by parents. Your students will be happy to see you at a Saturday event.

Drama productions take an immense amount of time, energy, and commitment. The drama department sometimes invites the students to a *teaser* of the upcoming evening production. It is a wise decision to go to the play that evening to support the students' hard work. They have worked several weeks to prepare for a play, and even though their parents will be attending the performance, it is always very special for students to see their teachers in the audience. You should also support musical performances, especially if your advisees are showcasing their talent in an evening performance.

Last but not least is the holiday party. The school sends an invitation by email – a few weeks in advance of the party. Be sure to RSVP via email. Not to respond to the invitation is rude and shows that you simply are not interested in being part of the social structure of the school community. Your attendance is required unless you have a major family issue (like a death in the family), which will supersede your being at this annual event. Dress appropriately. A jacket, shirt, and tie for men (no sneakers) and a party dress or a pants outfit for women will keep the fashion police at bay. It is the holiday season, so formal attire is expected. Also keep in mind that two drinks at a school function will suffice. Remember – as social as this event appears, it is sponsored by the school where you work. Be on your best behavior throughout the evening.

Attendance at all the previously mentioned social events is required. To be viewed as a teacher who goes beyond the classroom to support your students and colleagues at athletic, dramatic, and social events is the only way to have a long and successful career. If you choose not to extend your commitment to school functions beyond the classroom, you may be looking for a new job sooner rather than later. Mavericks have long been out of vogue.

CHAPTER 16

PROFESSIONAL GROWTH

Teachers need to be current regarding new trends in education. The best way to be up to date with methodology and best practices is to attend conferences either in a specific subject area or in general educational areas such as effective discipline, flexible scheduling, diversity in the classroom, or any topic related to improving the educational experience.

Often new teachers are reluctant to attend conferences because they think they should not be absent from the classroom; however, the benefits of going to conferences far outweigh teachers' absences for a day or even a few days. If classroom teachers leave organized lesson plans for substitute teachers (with requirements for written submissions for which students are accountable), the day(s) away from the classroom will be well spent for everyone. *Keeping current is not an option – it is essential.* Most schools require that teachers attend at least two conferences every year.

In lieu of one of the conferences, some principals will suggest that teachers visit classes at other schools in the area. Many great ideas often emerge from these visits. Teachers from other schools usually welcome these visits as long as they have a few weeks' notice about the date of your arrival.

Some teachers choose to return to college for higher-level degrees in the summer. Other teachers enjoy traveling to foreign countries to enrich their background for teaching in the upcoming year. Foreign travel is especially appropriate for teachers of foreign languages and history; however, teachers of all disciplines have the opportunity to apply for a summer sabbatical. If your school offers a mini-sabbatical (fee paid) for summer study, you should avail yourself of this opportunity. In order to participate in a summer sabbatical, you will have to submit a written overview of the trip, which explains how this newly, acquired knowledge will be integrated into the curriculum the following school year. The ultimate goal of a sabbatical is to improve and enrich the learning process for your students. Usually, several teachers will be awarded this opportunity to further their academic pursuits, which often includes travel, either domestic or foreign. Upon your return, you will be asked to give a presentation of your trip to the faculty, explaining the highlights of your educational experience. What a great way to spend a few weeks of your summer vacation!

Professional growth is a vital part of a school's budget – if the school is on the cutting edge of educational growth and development for its teachers. Having a vibrant faculty with new ideas that keep teaching exciting is worth every cent. Be sure to attend professional conferences yearly. The administration, parents, and students will thank you for your commitment to being the best teacher that you can be.

CHAPTER 17

EVALUATIONS

Evaluation of teachers is a standard procedure in all schools. An evaluation is not designed to be a punitive measure of your performance but rather a constructive method of assessing your strengths and weaknesses in the classroom. The evaluation will highlight your strengths as well as identify your weaknesses with strategies for improvement. It is very important that you are receptive to constructive criticism, both positive and negative, because this is how you will improve your teaching expertise.

The evaluation process begins during the opening faculty meetings. Since you will be one of the new teachers, everyone will be looking forward to meeting you and observing how you interact with your colleagues. It is always prudent to be polite and social while quietly listening and observing how procedures are done at your new school. The academic observations commence the first day of school when you meet your students and teach your first class of the year. It is very important that your daily performance is up to speed and consistent. You never know when your principal might make an unannounced visit to your classroom for a few, observational minutes. Be prepared.

In early October, you will be asked to set personal goals for the school year. Goals should be in the following areas: classroom management, professional growth, parent communication, a new pilot program in your subject area, or any area that you deem needs improvement. For example, you might have as a goal that you will attend five professional conferences during the academic year. Be careful how you write your goals because you will be evaluated on the quality and completion of them; the evaluation you receive will directly affect your contract and salary for the following year. In addition, your principal may add specific goals to your list of goals. For instance, if it is perceived that there is a general weakness among the faculty regarding attendance at afternoon games, a goal for required attendance may become a goal for all teachers.

Who observes you in the classroom? Usually, you will be observed at least two or three times each year. The head of the department for an academic discipline is best qualified to observe your knowledge of the subject and to assess how well you teach the curriculum. The principal also makes a classroom visit to observe your interaction with the students and to evaluate the methods you use to teach your class. These visits are scheduled for a specific date and time, so you will have time to prepare an excellent lesson. It is always a good idea to share your goals for the lesson with the evaluator – via email – ahead of time, so the necessary background of the unit and focus of the lesson are clearly understood. It is essential for an evaluator to have an overview of the entire unit, so the objectives of the unit and *how* the specific lesson is incorporated into the unit are clearly understood, prior to the observation. You will give yourself the best possible outcome by being thoroughly prepared and by preparing your evaluator in advance of the lesson.

What happens after the observations? Follow-up meetings will take place to discuss the lessons that were observed with the head of the department and with your principal. They will give specific feedback for the lesson they observed. Expect both positive and negative criticism because there is always room for improvement. All this information is documented in your school file, so if you disagree with a specific criticism, clearly explain what your goal was for the lesson and what was taught, from your perspective. Put this rebuttal in writing and ask to have this document added to your file. Should a problem arise in the future, it is always prudent to have your point of view documented regarding an observation.

Sometimes an observer does not have a thorough understanding of the goals of the lesson even though you have shared prior information for the observation. If you emailed the necessary information to your observer, and it was received in a timely manner, the following information should have been clearly stated before your observation: how the lesson is part of a larger unit, the goals of the specific lesson, and what role students will play in the lesson. Despite your best effort to explain the goals of your lesson, there still may be a miscommunication; therefore, it is prudent to invite an observer back for another observation, so you will have a second opportunity to demonstrate your expertise as an educator.

When all observations have been completed, you will be asked to sign a document that lists your goals and the principal's goal with evaluative ratings next to each goal. If some part of the evaluation, in your opinion, is not an accurate assessment of your professional performance, have your facts clearly typed for easy reference and be ready to dispute any misconceptions about your performance. A fair-minded principal will listen to your refutation. Then he or she will either agree with you or will state that there still remains a specific area that needs improvement. Most principals are willing to revisit a performance review document if factual information is presented, and you can demonstrate the veracity of your opinion. However, if there is one area that your principal still believes needs refinement, even after your presentation of the factual explanation, defer to your principal's judgment. The principal is ultimately in charge of the evaluation. Be sure to work on that one area of disagreement moving forward. Thank your principal for evaluating your performance and be sure to get a copy of the performance review for your records.

Evaluations require a great deal of time and effort from both the teacher and the evaluators. The performance review is a necessary procedure to evaluate whether or not a teacher is meeting the benchmarks of the profession. The majority of performance reviews are unbiased and objective, providing honest feedback and clear goals for the future. It is the rare instance when the opposite is the case. Overall, evaluations provide a measure of performance that will help teachers to become better educators.

CHAPTER 18
MOVING UP

Teaching is a profession that you either love or hate. It is not for everyone. Many people began a teaching career and then decided to leave and enter the business world. It takes a dedicated individual who likes to work with children and encourage them daily; the ultimate goal in teaching is to help students attain knowledge to the best of their ability with your guidance and support. Teaching is *not* an ego-driven profession but rather a caring profession that focuses on others – children and young adults. A teacher receives great satisfaction by working very hard each day with students; by the end of the year, the greatest reward is observing how much intellectual, emotional, and social growth has occurred. A successful year in teaching is measured by how much academic achievement, athletic and artistic accomplishments, and social and emotional maturity has occurred in one's students. It is amazing how much growth occurs in students in just one school year.

After three years in the profession, some teachers want to take on greater responsibility and leadership. How does a teacher pursue greater responsibility? The best way to take on more responsibility in most schools is to become the team leader or dean of a grade. The team leader will usually conduct class meetings, plan field trips, and attend weekly morning meetings with the principal and other team leaders from other grades. The school calendar, guest speakers, future school-wide activities, and any major issues facing the school are discussed. The dean is often the go-to person for all disciplinary issues in the grade that happen throughout the school day. This person has the most direct contact with a principal and weighs in on major disciplinary, academic, and social decisions for a particular grade. The dean position and the team leader position are both *add-on positions* to the usual teaching load; however, some schools allow these teachers who assume a team leader or a dean position to teach one less class, due to the time-intensive nature of these two positions. Most schools also pay a stipend for these positions. Either a team leader position or a dean position will be a good conduit to a more senior position such as dean of faculty or assistant principal. The administration will view you as an important member of the school community who is looking for career advancement.

Another way to continue to move up through the ranks is to put your hat in the ring to become the director of summer school. This position is a challenging one and is often filled by a teacher who plans to stay at a particular school for many years. Since the recruiting of students and teachers for summer school happens from December to May, the director of summer school has to do two jobs – teach and recruit simultaneously. Excellent organizational and communication skills are paramount if you are to be successful as a director.

When do most parents begin planning their summer schedules for their children? Since most parents work today, they begin planning summer activities for their children during the February break. Parents will be expecting the summer school schedules to be posted on the school website at that time or shortly thereafter. Once the advertisements are placed on the Internet via the school website and in local newspapers, the real work begins for the director.

What specific role does the director play to make summer school function seamlessly? The director has to make numerous phone calls to find prospective teachers for classes – if the regular faculty is not interested in teaching summer school. Other aspects of the job include the following: fielding calls from parents with inquiries about the daily schedule, discussing the specific classes that are offered (either for credit or enrichment), and explaining the different fees for lower, middle, and high school classes as well as possible payment options. This is the public relations part of the job. The director needs to convince parents that summer school has significant value, and that it is a unique opportunity for their children – not to be missed. Classes are offered not only for high school credit but also for remedial work; in addition, classes for enrichment in academic disciplines and improvement of athletic and drama skills are often popular choices for students in summer school. Students who have learning issues benefit significantly from attending summer school, so they do not lose the academic momentum that they have gained in a previous school year.

Sometimes the work of signing up students for summer school is coordinated with the school administrative assistant in the main office. However, the director does the majority of the work. If certain classes are not filled, then the cancellation calls must be made to inform parents that a particular class is undersubscribed and will not be offered.

There is also an athletic component to summer school, and this is often coordinated with the coaches at the school. The director registers a specific number of students per athletic offering, and the coach manages the day-to-day operation of the camps (soccer, baseball, lacrosse). These camps are great for students who want to improve their skills with a professional coach.

Finally, the daily, smooth functioning of the summer school rests on the shoulders of the director who handles any problems during the hours that the summer school is in session. With careful planning and dedicated teachers, summer school can be a fun experience for all involved.

If you decide that you would like to move from teaching in an independent school to a public school, there are several points to consider. First, I will address the negative points about a public school teaching position, and then I will comment on the positive points. In a public school, you will be teaching more students in each class, and the school year is about three weeks longer. You will need to be certified in the state in which you plan to teach. Most states require that you have a master's degree within five years of teaching in a particular state in order to obtain a permanent certificate. The curriculum is developed according to state standards; therefore, opportunities for creating your own curriculum are limited. There is not a great deal of professional support in a public institution. On the positive side of the equation, you do not have as many pressure-cooker parents who are demanding *concierge service* daily regarding their child's progress in your class. Your salary will be significantly improved as the years go by in a public school, especially if you have an advanced degree. You can also look forward to a comfortable retirement because public school pensions are much higher than those in independent schools.

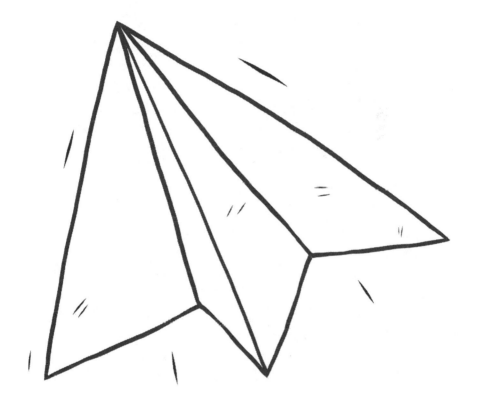

CHAPTER 19

BAD SITUATIONS

**Being defeated is often a temporary condition.
Giving up is what makes it permanent.
–Marilyn Vos Savant**

Most teaching situations are filled with teachable students, supportive colleagues, and understanding administrators. You will be given a teaching assignment when you initially sign a contract and then every June thereafter. That way you will be able to prepare and update your lessons during the summer for the upcoming school year. If you teach a subject that has heavy, reading content, it is necessary that you have time to read and prepare thoroughly – prior to the fall. Once the school year begins, there are several mandatory events such as Parents' Night, Open House, Conferences, as well as many more activities that will require your attendance and fill your days. Reading a chapter ahead of your students is no way to prepare lessons. It is pedagogically incorrect, and it will generate excessive anxiety, leaving no time for reflection about the material you are currently teaching. The writing and homework assignments you create for your new teaching schedule will be meaningful and challenging – only if you create them in advance during the summer months. Shooting from the hip never produces solid and impressive results. The old adage, "Success favors the prepared," is definitely true in teaching.

Once you have signed your yearly teaching contract, you should be professional and execute on your commitment. Sometimes your *bona fide* commitment can throw you an unexpected curve ball or two. Here are two situations that could occur after you have signed your contract. An additional course can be added to your teaching schedule in August – due to a hefty enrollment, or a coaching assignment may now be part of your schedule, requiring later afternoon departures and a competitive game schedule, which might also require Saturday games. These additional assignments are financially compensated, but the time commitment far exceeds for what you had initially planned. It is wise to comply with these requests for one academic year; however, if the expectations and added responsibilities prove to be too difficult to incorporate into your daily schedule, begin looking for a new job in February or March of that calendar year.

Looking for another teaching job while still employed is a challenge. Taking time off for interviews needs to be spread out, so you do not neglect your current students or give the appearance that you are actively looking for another job. Be sure to state to prospective employers that you want your inquiry to be absolutely confidential. Never let your current employer know that you are looking for a job. If you are about to be offered a contract later in the interview process, then give permission to your new, prospective employer to contact your current principal. Simply applying for a teaching job is never a guarantee of getting it, so be careful about your job search, always protecting your current teaching position – especially in an economic downturn. You may just have to teach another year at your current school, simply to remain employed.

I can remember being a seasoned teacher with undisputed loyalty when I was faced with an almost unbearable situation. I had taught English for many years, but due to an economic slowdown, there were not as many students to teach that year. I was asked to develop a new, creative writing curriculum and teach it to every student in the seventh grade. Teaching writing is a multi-step process, which involves many tedious hours of correcting in order to give appropriate feedback to students. After students have read the teacher's critiques of their essays and have made the necessary corrections to produce a final copy, their submissions require further correction by the teacher. My evenings and weekends were spent correcting essays nonstop for an entire year! In addition to teaching creative writing, I taught two English classes that year.

The next few years my schedule changed again to teach a combination of English classes and geography classes, heavily weighted in the subject that had more students to teach; I also taught an ethics class those years. These furiously, frenetic, four years are forever etched in my memory. I only endured these erratic, teaching assignments because the economy was dismal, and finally there was a portent of change after the fourth year of teaching in this manner. *Hope springs eternal!*

Fortunately, the principal found another job for the next academic year, and my teaching schedule stabilized. However, unless you like to teach a different discipline every year, I would not recommend your staying in such a situation. One only becomes proficient in teaching a discipline with dedication and experience. This leap frogging from one lily pad to another does not allow a teacher to become an expert in a discipline. One only learns what works well with students in a classroom by consistently teaching the same discipline, incorporating new research and best practices, and reflecting on what has been effective and what needs to be discarded. Therein lies the essence of masterful teaching.

As a young teacher, I embarked on a teaching career because I believed I could make a difference in the lives of young adults. I was completely committed to the profession. I taught English to one of the most social grades on the planet – seventh grade. My teaching assignment consisted of five classes with 30 students per class. Discipline was the daily focus. Since the principal's disciplinary policies were so loose and inconsistent, I had to require that the students who misbehaved in my classes remain after school for a detention, almost every day of the week – in order to retain some semblance of discipline. Between correcting piles of quizzes, tests, essays, and projects for 150 students and becoming the daily disciplinarian, I chose to leave the school after two years. I should have left after one year, but the popular view was that if you could not log in two years of teaching, your credibility was in question.

The incident that I will never forget was on the last day of my second year at this school. I wished everyone a wonderful summer. As I turned my back to face the blackboard for a few seconds, a rowdy student threw a huge wad of pink bubble gum in my hair! Roars of laughter ensued. That was the "crowning blow" that crystallized and reconfirmed I had made the correct decision to leave this school. When you find yourself in an impossible situation such as the following: no concrete disciplinary policies, no administrative support, no reasonable teaching assignment, and no change for the better in sight...it is time to depart. Fortunately, my future teaching assignments were significantly better, or I would not have lasted in the teaching profession for 35 years total, seven years in public school and 28 years in an independent school.

If you must remain in a bad teaching situation for financial reasons, continue to apply for new teaching positions. Remember that jobs are usually filled by April, so begin looking in February or March. The other option is to change professions. Many teachers have found other careers in sales and marketing. Teachers are born salespeople because they have been selling their discipline for years in the academic world. The main caveat is that now you will be working year round; furthermore, your vacation time will only be on long holiday weekends and two weeks of paid vacation, depending on the company's policy. This job change may have positive benefits because you will no longer be preparing lessons, correcting papers, logging in grades, and writing report cards. Your daily schedule may become more flexible, and you might even work from home occasionally. Working in business is a very different commitment, but it may be your best alternative if you do not believe you have the desire to teach any longer.

CHAPTER 20

TUTORING

Money, money, money! Teachers can supplement their income with tutoring after school, weekends, and summers. There is a significant demand for tutoring in all subject areas, study skills, ISEE/SSAT test preparation, SAT preparation, and college essays. An experienced teacher who has taught in a classroom knows the curriculum in a specific discipline far better than a random college graduate who works for a tutoring agency. Simply signing up with an agency will reduce your tutoring fee up to 50% after deducting the percentage taken by the tutoring agency. It is far more lucrative to find your own students and set your own fee for your services.

How do you go about finding students? First, you should let your principal know that you are interested in tutoring. Also, inform the guidance department about your interest in tutoring. Both sources get inquiries for tutors on a regular basis because they have the most direct contact with parents. Second, tell the parents of your students that you tutor; they will be happy to hear that a qualified, certified teacher is available for tutoring. The "parent grapevine" is a quick way to spread the word about your tutoring services. Third, create a business card and pass it out at the grocery store, at cocktail parties, and at parent conferences. Be sure to have the following information on your business card: your name, subjects that you teach, tests for which you prepare, your email address, and your phone number. Fourth, you might connect with a college placement agency whose main objective is to get students into the right college. These agencies are an excellent connection for tutoring. Students often have some academic deficiencies during their high school years, and a tutor is invaluable for teaching study skills and academic content during this time. Finally, you might choose to create a basic website to advertise your tutoring services.

Parents want to give their child the competitive edge in today's fast-paced world, and they are willing to pay for tutoring support. Tutoring support at a critical time – when a child is struggling with a particular subject – can make all the difference in a child's attitude toward the learning process and in achieving academic success. Difficulty in one subject can impact a student's performance in other subjects because a child's self-esteem is at risk. Especially during the teen years when the developing ego is so fragile, tutoring support is essential if a child is experiencing difficulty understanding a particular subject or needs to learn testing strategies to score well on a standardized test. No student wants to be mandated to make up a course in summer school, due to a failing grade in a required course. A student would much rather be tutored in a subject during the summer and then take a proficiency test in a specific subject – rather than attend summer school. Never underestimate the importance of your role as a tutor. You are the *lifeline* to help students perform at their optimum levels, gain confidence, and achieve academic success.

Preparation is essential to be a successful tutor. Contact the student's teacher by email or phone to obtain important information about the specific area in which the child is having difficulty. Get a copy of the text that the teacher is using for the course. Check the school website and keep apprised of the weekly assignments that the student has to complete. If there is a handout for a writing assignment or a project, ask for a copy of the instructions. Prior to a tutoring session, create worksheets, graphic organizers, and informational handouts that will create a focus for the tutoring session. Remember that you are the anchor for the child in a storm of confusion about a particular subject.

Where does the tutoring take place? Libraries are a popular location for tutoring. You will find that most libraries are happy to accommodate tutors, and some libraries have study rooms that can be booked one week in advance of your tutoring session. Other libraries actually charge a quarterly fee for you to tutor at their facilities. Try to avoid these libraries if possible. Some students are tutored at school locations where a teacher teaches during the day – after school hours. I have even seen students being tutored at Starbucks coffee shops and Panera restaurants. Personally, I do not think coffee shops and local eateries are the ideal locations for tutoring, but they may be *as good as it gets* – given the particular circumstances. Try to avoid tutoring at a child's home or at your home, unless you have a firm exit plan. Parents tend to try to tap your brain for all kinds of advice after the tutoring session is finished. You could be asked a question about technology (cellphones, the Internet, etc.) or how to deal with an emotional problem with their child. This is time-consuming and exhausting.

Payment is a whole other issue. Since tutoring agencies book one month in advance, some parents will try to pay you at the end of the month. Never accept this arrangement. Once I was not paid for an entire month of weekly tutoring sessions and had to send multiple bills with follow-up phone calls to finally collect for my services. I learned through the college of hard knocks how not to be paid. Ask for payment each time you tutor, preferably in cash or by check. Cash the check immediately; if there is a problem, you will know to insist on cash for the next session. Remember a parent would never go to Starbucks and ask if they could pay for eight lattes at the end of the month! Establish this payment arrangement on the phone or in person upon accepting a tutoring job. It will save you valuable time and prevent future frustration.

I have been paid in cash in many different ways. The most respectful way to be paid is when a parent puts the cash in an envelope and hands it to you or has the child hand the envelope to you. There have been occasions when parents became "absent minded" upon paying the fee for tutoring and tried to cut the price by five or ten dollars, even though the fee was clearly discussed on the phone – prior to the first session. You simply have to count the money and state clearly that the fee is what you had discussed – not a penny less. Do not be intimidated by this kind of behavior.

The most memorable payment, however, was when I was paid by a high-powered, shipping magnate; he pulled out a roll of bills from his pocket and asked how much he owed me. I was taken aback at first, but I quickly regained my composure, realizing that he was comfortable doing business this way. I clearly stated the fee we had agreed upon, and I took the money from his hand. This is how I was paid in subsequent tutoring sessions, and he never missed a payment.

I advertised my tutoring services at a local library on a community website. The community organization was located in the library but was not affiliated with the library. I thought this would be a viable way to find students to tutor. I had one parent respond to my advertisement. The parent via email said his sixteen-year-old daughter was coming from Sweden to America for a three-week holiday, and he wanted her to be tutored in English. She did not speak very much English but understood the language if spoken clearly and slowly. I emailed back and told him that I would be happy to work with his daughter; this would be more of an ESL assignment, for which I had previous experience. I emailed back the dates, times, and location of the tutoring sessions, which would take place in the library. I thought all the necessary information for the tutoring sessions was clearly communicated.

Now here is the rub. Then I received another email from the father stating that he and his wife were proponents of education; he worked for the military in Switzerland, and his wife was a reporter. Wait a moment! I thought his daughter, who was sixteen years old, was from Sweden. Then he proceeded to tell me that he would send a large check for the tutoring, which I would deposit in my bank account. I would take my fee for the tutoring, and then pay the nanny, the taxi driver and her lodging. He also wanted my full name, email address (which he already had) and my phone number. Something was clearly rotten in the state of Switzerland!

I quickly realized that this was a scam, so I sent an email that firmly stated, "I am not available to tutor your daughter in August." There was no further communication between us because the con artist clearly knew that I had detected his ruse. Therefore, be very suspicious of any inquiry for tutoring that may have any inkling of a scam.

CHAPTER 21
RANDOM ADVICE

This information did not fit in any of the preceding chapters, but I felt it was worth mentioning. These are tips that will help you to be more successful in your teaching career.

1. **School Lunches.** I would suggest that you pack your lunch a few days of the week. You can easily bring some healthy sandwiches such as: turkey, chicken, ham, or tuna with a bottle of water and a piece of fruit (apple, orange, peach). Friday pizza may be fine; however, after a short time you may be packing on unwelcomed pounds. Teenagers whisk away the calories from chicken nuggets, pasta, and tacos, but this daily diet for adults is not an option. If you happen to have a salad bar at your school, this is great choice to mix with your bagged-lunch sandwiches. Eating a healthy diet is essential for sustained energy and razor-like focus.

2. **Fun Fridays and Holidays**. Your advisees will look forward to Fridays if you bring in some goodies on that day. Some suggestions are a box of *Dunkin Donuts*, a few packages of *Oreo* cookies, or *Pepperidge Farm* chocolate chip cookies. These goodies do not cost very much money, and they will put a sparkle into Fridays. For the holiday season, purchase candy canes; on Valentine's Day, buy some *Hershey's Kisses* or heart candies with words; and at Easter, buy a few bags of *M&M's* with spring colors. These will be the moments your advisees will remember.

3. **Halloween**. If your school allows costumes for Halloween, dress for the occasion and be part of the activity. One year I wore a homemade costume for which I actually won a prize. It was a dyed-green sheet wrapped around my body with a Statue of Liberty foam hat, and I carried a torch. Another year I was Static Cling; I dressed in a black turtleneck with black pants. Then I pinned dryer sheets and a variety of colored socks on my turtleneck and pants. However, the best costume I ever wore was when I was the Queen of Hearts; I wore two poster boards with the Queen of Hearts on the front and the back (drawn from the queen card in a deck of cards). Fortunately, my sister was an art teacher who offered her artistic talent to draw the posters. Finally, if you cannot think of a costume, you can always be a traditional witch with a black hat and a black cape. Add some striped stockings for pizzazz. No matter what costume you decide to wear, students will be happy you participated in Halloween.

4. **Exercise and Sleep**. Exercise is essential to remain physically and emotionally healthy. It will also help you to de-stress from the demands of teaching. You owe it to yourself to get a minimum of a half hour of brisk walking – three times a week, either on a treadmill or outside in the fresh air. Add some weights to your workout for even greater healthful benefits. The exercise will keep you fit and will clear your head from the day's events. Exercising more often will bring even greater healthy results. Getting seven or eight hours of sleep is absolutely necessary to meet the demands of the long school days. Be disciplined and get the proper amount of sleep each night. (Record all those late television shows for weekend viewing.) You will be at your optimum performance with the required hours of sleep each night.

5. **Parking**. You will most likely be assigned a parking spot at your school. Park there with one caveat; during baseball

season, move your car to another location if your assigned spot is near the baseball field. Ironically, I can remember seeing the baseball coach's back windshield smashed by a stray baseball. He felt confident that a stray ball would never come near the cars parked by the field because there was a high net placed behind home base to catch them. Unfortunately, stray balls have a way of finding their way to parked cars in their locale. To avoid calling your auto insurance company with a *tale of woe*, park far away from the baseball field by moving your car after school dismissal.

6. **Valuables**. Be prudent and lock your pocketbook or wallet in a file cabinet or in the trunk of a locked car. Then carry your car keys on your person using a key chain or place them in your pocket throughout the day. Never leave your car keys or room keys on a desk; they must always be in your pocket or on a key chain for safety purposes.

7. **Proctoring**. During the school year, there will be opportunities to proctor students who are taking the ISEE/SSAT tests to get into independent schools. Other students will be taking AP Exams, which will also require proctors. Teachers are given a stipend for proctoring each of these tests or exams. Proctoring is a good way for teachers to supplement their income.

CHAPTER 22

LAST DAY

When assessments are handed back to the students for review, and final grades are shared, it is time for the Closing Ceremony. Prior to the day of the ceremony, a few rehearsals will have taken place, so students will learn how to make a proper entrance and exit into the outdoor tent or into an auditorium during the day of the ceremony. Students are looking forward to their summer vacation, but first they must be respectful and honor the new graduates of the middle school. The students in sixth grade and seventh grade are looking forward to moving into the next grade. It is one of the most exciting days of students' lives, knowing that they have moved up to the next level of their educational journey.

During the ceremony, deans of a grade will sit with the entire grade to be sure the students are attentive and act appropriately during the ceremony. Other teachers will sit near the stage. The eighth grade students are the *stars* of the ceremony because they will be receiving their diplomas, which signify their graduation from middle school – a very emotional and exciting day. Girls wear their lovely dresses, and boys don blazers, shirts, ties, and grey pants to celebrate their special day. The day is bittersweet because students are looking back on their three years of wonderful experiences in middle school as well as anticipating their future experiences in the high school. The experience is formal and very memorable.

Parents who are in the audience for the ceremony may personally thank you for a great year and sometimes give you a gift. Be gracious and politely accept their compliments for a job well done. If you do receive a gift, a personal thank you is the proper protocol. As old-fashioned as it may seem, I advocate sending a handwritten, thank-you note. If you are overwhelmed with too many other responsibilities and cannot write a handwritten note, a very thankful email will suffice. Never text a thank you as that is thankless and rude, even in today's society.

As I mentioned in the earlier chapters, in order to become a successful teacher, you need expertise, compassion, and commitment. You will never become rich by worldly standards, but you will be rich with amazing memories when you retire. Teaching is not for the faint of heart; it is for those who have the courage and dedication to prepare students with the knowledge and values that will prepare them for a lifetime.

CHAPTER 23
CONCLUSION

A teacher affects eternity; he can never
tell where his influence stops.
–Henry Adams

Teaching is a profession that affects the lives of thousands of young minds during the course of one's career. Great teachers not only teach but also inspire and create a love of learning. There are many subjects that students must learn in the course of their academic school life. Teachers who challenge, support, and guide them throughout the learning process will make them excited about the quest for more knowledge. Learning should become a lifelong pursuit.

Technology has enhanced the learning process in education today. It has opened the modes of communication. Students can now write, revise, and rewrite their essays more thoroughly with computers. Simulations of biology, chemistry, and physics experiments on computers have brought depth and scope to students' understanding of the sciences. Primary sources for history papers are easy to access using the Internet and can be incorporated into dialectical analyses. Foreign languages can be taught and reinforced with follow-up lessons on the Internet; practicing pronunciation of foreign words is now easier for students by using textbook-connected, computer programs. Artistic creations and musical compositions can also be created with Internet programs. It is a whole new world with a myriad of possibilities for teachers to expand the scope and depth of knowledge they impart to their students. Teachers are also facilitators of learning by directing students to the best websites; students then can use these websites to research the material they need for presentations, papers, and projects. Teachers of all disciplines must become aware of the endless possibilities that the Internet offers in order to develop and improve their lessons in the classroom.

Every summer, teachers should evaluate what worked well in their classroom and what needs tweaking for the next academic year. Lessons should never become stale and out of date. Excellent teachers use the summer months to create new and challenging lessons for the following year. It serves a dual purpose; teachers are enthusiastic about teaching an updated curriculum, and the students are the recipients of state-of-the-art information.

The class that I referred to at the beginning of this book was the last class that I taught after 28 years in an independent school. They were the most delightful group of students to teach because they were cooperative and respectful throughout the entire school year. Of course, they pulled some clever ruses to leave the classroom or surf the Internet at inappropriate times, but once they were warned to stop, they did. This class as a whole had an incredible moral compass; credit for this good behavior is directly linked to the conscientious, child-rearing techniques used by their parents. I was fortunate to have my final year of teaching be such a rewarding one. Teaching has its own intangible rewards that affect not only the heart but also the soul of both the students and the teacher.

APPENDIX

Preparation Checklist

1. ☐ Unpack the new books and record the numbers in your grade book and on a computer sheet.
2. ☐ Place inspirational posters and academic posters on the walls of your classroom.
3. ☐ Prepare folders for your advisees and place them in a large, plastic box near your desk.
4. ☐ Place a bulletin board in the front of the room and post important announcements.
5. ☐ Hang a large calendar in the front of your classroom.
6. ☐ Fill a large, plastic box with lined paper, pencils, pens, rulers, a stapler, and 3x5 notecards for student use.
7. ☐ Prepare a substitute lesson and place it in a folder.
8. ☐ List the names of your students in your grade book and keep records in both your grade book and on the computer.
9. ☐ Arrange your desks in one of the following styles: seminar, rectangular, or traditional (row-by-row).
10. ☐ Learn your students' names. Use last year's yearbook to connect faces to names.
11. ☐ Post your homework on the school website.
12. ☐ Prepare and print a copy of the classroom rules; post them on the bulletin board.
13. ☐ Print out an expectations sheet, which gives an overview of your course and the disciplinary rules for the classroom. Ask students to sign this handout and also have their parents sign it – to be returned to you the next day. Save this document for the entire year.
14. ☐ Get a good night's sleep prior to the first day of school, eat a hearty breakfast, and arrive at school with a smile on your face and a positive attitude.

Parents' Night Checklist

1. ☐ Prepare the following handouts: course syllabus, grading policy, and disciplinary rules. Create printed copies and place them in piles on your desk.
2. ☐ Create a script for the evening. The script should include the following: a friendly welcome and a thank you to the parents for coming to Parents' Night, an introduction about yourself, an overview of your course, your disciplinary policy, and your email for further communication.
3. ☐ Use a whiteboard marker and write your email on the whiteboard.
4. ☐ Cut and paste your typed script on *large note cards* for easy retrieval of the information for your speech.
5. ☐ Place your texts for the year on your desk and hold them up when you are mentioning a specific part of your course (for example, hold up a copy of the play that you are currently teaching – *A Midsummer Night's Dream* by William Shakespeare – and talk about the importance of that genre in your curriculum.)
6. ☐ Organize the desks or tables in your room for the easiest traffic flow.
7. ☐ Clean your desks with Windex and pick up any papers on the floor. All your whiteboards should be clean. Be sure your room sparkles!
8. ☐ Dress appropriately for the evening. Women should wear a suit, a blouse with pants, or a sweater with a skirt. Heels or flats should accompany the outfit with conservative accessories such as a watch and a necklace. Men should wear a suit or a sport coat with a shirt and tie

accompanied by a pair of dress pants and shoes. Sneakers are never appropriate for Parents' Night.

9. ☐ Rehearse your speech several times to make a great first impression.

Field Trips Checklist

1. ☐ Check the school calendar to be sure you have chosen a day on which no other activities have been scheduled.
2. ☐ Call the business office of the museum, campsite, or theater to make reservations for your trip. Discuss payment procedures.
3. ☐ Make a reservation with the bus company for your trip. Be sure to discuss the date, as well as the departure time and return time for the trip. Discuss payment procedures.
4. ☐ Ask the school accountant for checks to take with you on the trip; otherwise, ask the accountant to mail checks via the USPS or send them electronically.
5. ☐ Be sure you have enough chaperones; one chaperone for every ten students is usually required.
6. ☐ Check that all permission slips and contact information are either in a database, which can be accessed via a cellphone, or assign a teacher to bring the paper copies for the trip.
7. ☐ Contact the cafeteria to let them know how many bag lunches you will need for the day of the trip.
8. ☐ Instruct students to *always* stay in their advisory groups before they leave the school campus. *No student ever goes anywhere alone.* Repeat these instructions again before students get off the bus at the trip location.
9. ☐ Ask advisors if all their advisees have boarded the bus. Then do a total roll call of the entire class to double check that all students are on the bus. Give the head count to the bus driver.
10. ☐ Upon arrival at your destination, instruct students to get into their advisory groups. State that they will remain in their advisory groups at all times for the duration of the trip.

11. ☐ Do a head count for each advisory group before the students go into a museum, campsite, theater, or any trip location.
12. ☐ Inspect students' duffle bags, if it is a camp trip, and confiscate all candy and gum, so no "hungry critters" can raid your cabins in the evening.
13. ☐ Upon departing from a trip location, take an advisory head count and a total roll call of the entire class again to be sure no child is left behind.

Conferences Checklist

1. ☐ Supervise your advisees to be sure they are filing their quizzes, tests, and projects in their designated folders, which are located in a plastic box in your classroom.
2. ☐ Create academic goals with each of your advisees (for example, Goal: Attend help sessions in math – prior to tests.)
3. ☐ Discuss academic progress with your advisees once a week or at least every two weeks. Review quizzes, tests, and projects in their portfolios and suggest strategies to improve their performance.
4. ☐ Xerox a copy of your advisees' report cards and highlight in yellow the positive and negative comments from their teachers – prior to the conferences in November.
5. ☐ Check to see if the parents of your advisees have signed up on the school website for a conference. If they have not signed up – *two weeks before the conference date* – call to remind them that conferences are being held on a specific date. Suggest that they select a conference time on the website that works for them because it is very important to discuss their child's progress to date.
6. ☐ Conduct pre-conferences with your advisees about two weeks before the conference date. Help them organize their work by date and subject; then discuss their progress to date. Ask your advisees in what subjects they need to improve and offer suggestions to help them perform at a higher level of achievement in the future.
7. ☐ Greet parents and your advisees with a welcoming, "Hello, and thank you for coming today." Shake hands with the parents and your advisees. Have all your highlighted report cards, advisees' academic folders, and a notepad for

important information that will be discussed during the conferences.

8. ☐ Make it clear from the beginning of the conference that you are there to discuss the positive and negative aspects of the child's performance this past trimester; the ultimate goal is to discuss strategies for improvement in the next trimester. Positivity is necessary for future success!

9. ☐ Be supportive of your advisees' efforts. Never let them be discouraged by a bad grade. Suggest that advisees who are having difficulty in an academic subject attend after-school help sessions.

10. ☐ Suggest to parents that a tutor may be necessary to help students who have already been attending extra help sessions regularly, without improvement. Sometimes students who have serious gaps in a subject need the support of a tutor to target the problem and remediate it.

11. ☐ Shake hands with the parents and your advisees at the end of the conferences. State that your email is the best way to discuss academic progress or concerns in the future.

12. ☐ Stay on schedule with your conferences. Parents should not have to wait more than five extra minutes for their scheduled conferences. Sit facing the clock in your room, so you will be cognizant of the passage of time.

End of Year Checklist

1. ☐ Collect all hardcover books and store them in a locked closet.
2. ☐ Send a list of students' names who have lost their books to the administrative assistant, so a bill can be sent to their parents.
3. ☐ Submit book orders for next fall to the school administrative assistant. Keep a copy for your files.
4. ☐ Clean out student desks and lockers. Save any unused markers, pens, notebooks, binders, and post-it notes for next year; students who cannot afford these supplies will be appreciative of your recycling.
5. ☐ Remove all valuables from your desk and store them in a locked, file cabinet.
6. ☐ Clean all tables and desks with a disinfectant cleaner. Take down any posters or paintings that are valuable and store them in a safe place.
7. ☐ Erase and clean all whiteboards. Remember to also clean the trays.
8. ☐ Organize your files (paper and electronic). Cleaning your files before the beginning of summer vacation will give you a fresh start in the fall.
9. ☐ Store your computer, wireless units, and presentation systems with the technology department.
10. ☐ Be sure all your report card obligations have been met before you leave for summer vacation.
11. ☐ Create a summer "to do" list. Read the required, educational book if your school system requires it. Revisit your course syllabus and update it for the next school year.
12. ☐ Leave your cellphone number and email with your principal, so you can be contacted during the summer months – if necessary.

Resources

"Albert Einstein Quotes." BrainyQuote. Accessed July 1, 2015. http://www.brainyquote.com/quotes/authors/a/ albert_einstein.html.

"Alexander Graham Bell Quotes." BrainyQuote. Accessed July 1, 2015. http://www.brainyquote.com/quotes/authors/a/ alexander_graham_bell.html.

"Anti-Bullying Bill Becomes Law - Connecticut General Assembly." July 13, 2011. Accessed October 16, 2015. http://www.cga.ct.gov/coc/PDFs/bullying/2011_bullying_law.pdf.

Borkar, Rujuta. "Pros and Cons of Using Cell Phones in School." Buzzle. January 5, 2012. Accessed August 15, 2015. http://www.buzzle.com/articles/cell-phones-in-school-pros-and-cons-html.

"Buddha Quotes." BrainyQuote. Accessed July 01, 2015. http://www.brainyquote.com/quotes/authors/b/buddha.html.

"C. S. Lewis Quotes." BrainyQuote. Accessed July 01, 2015. http://www.brainyquote.com/quotes/authors/c/c_s_lewis.html.

"Definition of Cyberbullying in English:." Cyberbullying. Accessed July 01, 2015. http://www.oxforddictionaries.com/definition/english/cyberbullying.

"English Idioms Daily Blog." The Apple Does Not Fall Far from the Tree. Accessed July 01, 2015. http://www.english-idioms.com/index_files/the-apple-does-not-fall-from-the-tree.html.

"Excuses at FinestQuotes.com." FinestQuotes. Accessed July 01, 2015. http://www.finestquotes.com/select_quote-category-Excuses-page-1.html.

"Henry Adams Quotes." BrainyQuote. Accessed July 01, 2015. http://www.brainyquote.com/quotes/authors/h/henry_adams.html.

"Henry Ford Quotes." BrainyQuote. Accessed July 01, 2015. http://www.brainyquote.com/quotes/authors/h/henry_ford.html.

"Marilyn Vos Savant Quotes." BrainyQuote. Accessed July 01, 2015. http://www.brainyquote.com/quotes/authors/m/marilyn_vos_savant.html.

Meador, Derrick. "Cellphones in Schools: Embrace Them or Ban Them." February 25, 2015. Accessed July 1, 2015. http://teaching.about.com/od/admin/f/Embrace-Cell-Phones-Or-Ban-Them.html.

Rochman, Bonnie. "School Security: Why It's So Hard to Keep Kids Safe | TIME.com." Time. December 18, 2012. Accessed August 19, 2015. http://healthland.time.com/2012/12/18/school-security-why-its-so-hard-to-keep-kids-safe/.

"Theodore Roosevelt Quotes." BrainyQuote. Accessed June 29, 2015. http://www.brainyquote.com/quotes/authors/t/theodore_roosevelt.html.

"What Is Bullying?" Accessed November 28, 2015. http://www.stopbullying.gov/what-is-bullying/index.html.

45727589R00085

Made in the USA
Lexington, KY
18 July 2019